Wicked Problems, Righteous Solutions

Wicked Problems, Righteous Solutions

A Catalogue of
Modern
Software Engineering Paradigms

Peter DeGrace
and
Leslie Hulet Stahl

YOURDON PRESS
Prentice Hall Building
Englewood Cliffs, New Jersey 07632

Library of Congress Cataloging-in-Publication Data

DeGrace, Peter.
    Wicked problems, righteous solutions : a catalogue of modern
software engineering paradigms / by Peter DeGrace and Leslie Hulet
Stahl.
        p.   cm.
    Includes bibliographical references.
    ISBN 0-13-590126-X
    1. Software engineering.   I. Stahl, Leslie Hulet.   II. Title.
QA76.758.D44   1991
005.1--dc20   90-32238
                                                               CIP

Editorial/production supervision
  and interior design: Laura A. Huber
Cover design: Leslie Hulet Stahl
Manufacturing buyer: Kelly Behr

Figures 6-1, 6-4, 6-5 and 6-6 photos
  courtesy of David Finn.
Clip art is used by permission of
  T/Maker Company.
ClickArt® is a registered trademark
  of T/Maker Co.©, 187.

 © 1990 by Prentice-Hall, Inc.
A Division of Simon & Schuster
Englewood Cliffs, New Jersey 07632

The publisher offers discounts on this book when ordered
in bulk quantities. For more information, write:

    Special Sales/College Marketing
    College Technical and Reference Division
    Prentice Hall
    Englewood Cliffs, New Jersey 07632

Printed in the United States of America

10 9 8 7 6 5 4 3

ISBN 0-13-590126-X

Prentice-Hall International (UK) Limited, *London*
Prentice-Hall of Australia Pty. Limited, *Sydney*
Prentice-Hall Canada Inc., *Toronto*
Prentice-Hall Hispanoamericana, S.A., *Mexico*
Prentice-Hall of India Private Limited, *New Delhi*
Prentice-Hall of Japan, Inc., *Tokyo*
Simon & Schuster Asia Pte. Ltd., *Singapore*
Editora Prentice-Hall do Brasil, Ltda., *Rio de Janeiro*

DEDICATIONS

This book is dedicated to all the "real" programmers who helped me move from being a novice to being a journeyman programmer, especially Gary Shurtleff; to all of my correspondents; to our resident "shark," Lisa Scott, for believing in us and waiting for her check; to my teacher, John Bush; and, especially, to my friend Dave Holladay, who believed that I could do it.

Peter DeGrace

To my parents (hi Mom!), who taught me that anything is possible as long as you work hard enough; to my husband, David M. Stahl, for his patience, endurance, love, and our encapsulated universe; and to my partner, Peter DeGrace, without whom (obviously) this dedication would not have been possible: Thanks, guys, I needed that!

Leslie Hulet Stahl

CONTENTS

ILLUSTRATIONS

Wicked Problems, Righteous Solutions

INTRODUCTION

This book is the result of a collaboration between two authors. Each author has brought to the project their own unique set of skills and expertise. However, we wrote the book from Peter's perspective because the views and opinions are his. So, we use "I" in the discussions instead of "we."

❖❖❖

In my time as a programmer, I have seen many ways of doing programming, and some are more formal than others. I have also noticed that when programmers follow the "official" way, things often don't go very well. When things *do* go well, it is often because the programmers didn't follow the "official" way.

Both cases have caused a lot of confusion and, I guess guilt, in me and my colleagues. Therefore, I decided to investigate the ways we do programming in the hope of clearing up the confusion and relieving the guilt. But, before I got very far, I stumbled into the "state of our art." I discovered that our profession is not like other professions. In order to proceed, I needed to understand more about us programmers and our field. This book is the result. It is a catalog, of sorts, about the methods we use and the ways in which we do programming. It is *not* a catechism of a "right way" or the "true faith."

Instead, I am going to address the *nature* of problem solving by examining how we organize ourselves to do our work. This process is sometimes called a *methodology*, but that term is misleading and is often misused. The term connotes a lot of things and activities.

In the software engineering environments I have experienced, we have defined a *methodology* as the models (paradigms), management practices, technical practices, tools, and training procedures used to produce software. Each of these items is drawn from a fairly large pool of resources. Even though it is big, this definition has the virtue of making it possible to compare apples with apples and oranges with

1

oranges. For example, one would compare the applicability of the data flow diagrams from structured analysis with HIPO (Hierarchical Input Process Output) charts (since both are technical practices) rather than with Gantt Charts (which is a management practice).

Table 1 is a listing of some popular management and technical practices. I won't discuss them in detail here, but they are described in the existing literature. (Incidentally, there is an excellent description of the technical practices in Martin's book, *Diagramming Techniques for Analysts and Programmers.* [Martin and McClure 1985])

Table 1. Some Management and Technical Practices

Management Practices	Technical Practices (continued)
Control Rooms	Trees and Decision Tables
Unit Development Folders	State Transition Diagrams
Program Notebooks	Data Structure Diagrams
Charts	Entity Relationship Diagrams
Documents	Data Navigation Diagrams
	Compound Data Accesses
Technical Practices	Guide to Programming Techniques
Decomposition Diagrams	Process Modelling
Dependency Diagrams	Yourdin
Data Flow Diagrams	DeMarco
Functional Decomposition	Constantine
Structure Charts	Gane and Sarson
HIPO Diagrams	PSI
Warnier Orr Diagrams	Data Driven
Michael Jackson Diagrams	Warnier/Orr Diagrams
Flow Charts	Michael Jackson
Structured English and Pseudocode	Flavin, Chen, and Martin
Nassi-Schneiderman Charts	Object Oriented
Action Diagrams	Booch Diagrams

The composition of each of the categories in a methodology isn't perfectly clear yet, and I have made some decisions about what should comprise some of them. For example, the Jackson Design Method and Object Oriented Programming are frequently referred to as methodologies. [Case 1987] However, they're not, in my view, complete yet, so I classify them as technical practices—as ways of mapping the problem space into a solution space or decomposing problems into manageable chunks.

There are five classes of models. The first is the Waterfall model, which is the well-known model that many of us have used for development work up until now. It seems to be the most written about, and is based on top-down development and an ordered set of activities that are performed in sequence.

The second class comprises some variations on the Waterfall and Incremental models. The Incremental models come from both Barry Boehm [Boehm 1981] and from one of my correspondents. I will also discuss Boehm's new Spiral model [Boehm 1985] as part of this class.

The third class encompasses the Prototyping models. I will discuss five of them: (1) prototyping to achieve better requirements, (2) simulation, which is a variation on this theme, (3) prototyping as application development itself, (4) prototyping as operational specifications, and (5) transformational prototyping.

The fourth class contains the All-at-Once models, including Scrum, Handcuff, and Hacking in the best sense of the word.

Then, there is a miscellaneous class in which there are four models: (1) Video, (2) Cleanroom, (3) End-User Development, and (4) System Engineering.

❖❖❖

This book is especially for my colleagues who are currently working to make computers useful. It should help you to understand the "state of our art," or at least my view of it (Chapters One, Two, and Nine); the methods we use to "do" programming, from the formal to the *very* informal (Chapters Three, Five, Six, Seven, and Eight); and some of the problems associated with orthodoxy (Chapter Four). I hope you enjoy it and find it enlightening.

The title of this book reflects, I'm sorry to say, a condition of our field where there are often more moral issues than technical ones. That is why I have chosen the term "wicked" to describe a certain set of problems that involve not only large and complex problems of a technical nature, but also problems of a moral nature. This book provides some righteous solutions to these wicked problems.

I have collected information from many associates who I refer to as correspondents. They work in many different areas for many companies, and some are in business for themselves. I have used their information in two ways. Mostly I would hear some remarkable statement, remember it, and use it here to accent information from the literature. But, sometimes I would use it to verify material from the literature that seemed a little doubtful.

Although I have organized the ideas in this book in a new way, most of them are not new. You might find that the organization could be different or that some information is just plain wrong. If you do, I would like to hear from you. One of the benefits about trying to be scientific is that you are entitled to be just plain wrong (not often, one hopes) and not be burned at the stake. So, if I'm wrong about the way I organized the information or if any of the ideas are incorrect, then tell me about it. There is a mailer in the back of the book.

Now, I will start this tour by discussing Science, Software Engineering, and the context of our work. This might seem like an unnecessary digression, but there are some ideas to be presented that will lead into the heart of the matter. So, please bear with me.

CHAPTER ONE
Software Engineering and Science

The field of software engineering is just struggling into existence. It is more of a craft than an engineering discipline because it is not based on science. Like the craft guilds that built the great cathedrals of Europe in the Middle Ages, our field has grown through trial and error, experience, practice, and the molding of practices into procedures.

This is not to say that programming has no association with science and engineering; indeed, the first programmers were engineers. In addition, hypotheses are made and tested, and checked out by laboratory, field, and survey studies. This gives the illusion of science. However, investigators looking at the state of the science have this to say:

" ... structured programming theory is in a sorry state and this becomes more apparent when we examine ... the status of structured programming hypotheses." [Vessey and Weber 1984, p.398]

I believe this is because we have no *native* theory of our own.

Larry Constantine, one of the leaders in the field of structured design, traced the development of the craft of software engineering in the preface to his book, *Structured Design*, in which he states, "Somehow, despite or even because of the constant fire-fighting in cranking out routine business applications we found time to think and talk about what we were doing. The earliest 'investigations' of program structure to which I often refer were no more than noon-hour critiques of each others' programs and long afternoon debates of what might have been done differently to avoid difficulties we encountered in debugging, maintaining or modifying our programs." [Yourdon and Constantine 1977]

His experiences and discussions led to structured design and some pretty good rules of thumb about programming, but not insight into *what* we program about (data, information, and knowledge) nor

5

how we program (what really goes on when we write code). Neither has it led into any explanation about how the world works—about Nature.

Science has made dramatic advances. The builders during the Middle Ages were able to produce no more than several hundred great cathedrals throughout Europe. With their trial-and-error processes, they produced an improved arch and flying buttresses to better transmit and support the loads of the great weight of stone, and made the production of large, stained-glass windows possible. With scientific advances in architectural design and with materials such as steel and aluminum, we now have cities filled with cathedral-sized structures, and *most* of them have their entire exteriors covered with windows.

Science provides an agreed-upon vocabulary wherein everyone agrees on *what* the words mean, though not necessarily on *where* they can be applied. For example, the "Big Bang" theory is understood by all cosmologists, even though they don't all agree that it is the appropriate term with which to describe the beginning of the universe. But, the field of software engineering doesn't have an agreed-upon vocabulary. For example, *object-oriented programming* has many definitions. [See *Byte*, August 1986, p. 139]

The same is true of the following terms: architecture (which is used everywhere, all the time), information hiding, reusable code, methodology, binary, paradigm, word, and application. In fact, many of us don't even agree on the name of our field. In business environments, it was originally called *data processing*. Now it is called *information processing*. In engineering environments, it is called *computing*. Now, some of us even want to change the name again, to *knowledge processing*.

The tools and procedures used in a field of science are understood by everyone in that field. For example, it would be extraordinary to encounter a physicist who achieved that status without ever encountering a balanced beam scale or a description of how to use one. But, the tools and procedures of the craft guilds of the Middle Ages varied from locale to locale. What was permissible in one city was often prohibited in another. Even though some uniformity was accomplished, especially by stone masons and other itinerant workers who took their skills with them from place to place, much was influenced by local customs and superstitions, such as the craft of ironworking.

The tools and procedures of software engineering vary just as those of the craft guilds did. Some software shops use flow charts and others use data flow diagrams. Different programming shops use different languages, different versions of the same language, or invent their own language. And, they use a variety of programming tools that are often incompatible with other programming tools, such as text and graphics that cannot be read by text editors or do not provide output in a form than can be read by text editors.

Science supports engineering with theories of how the world works. Software engineering has no supporting theory. We have no formulae such as the famous e=Mc². (There is something called information theory, but it is really a telecommunications idea that describes how much data can be transmitted through a conductor.)

Here are some comments from Susan Lammers book, *Programmers at Work* [1986] that were made by some pretty eminent folks in our field when they were asked whether computer science is Science:

"... I don't know what truth computer science is trying to learn." [ibid, p.55]

"It will be ..." [ibid, p.81]

"I definitely consider (programming) to be an art." [ibid, p.201]

"... I call (computer science) a craft because it certainly isn't a science yet." [ibid, p.216]

Science provides engineering with reliable data about *things*, such as accurate, consistent descriptions of natural elements. Science needs this data to establish the existence of these elements in the first place. This information results from empirically testing hypotheses after systematically and objectively collecting data about nature, which is the scientific method. It is difficult to obtain reliable, repeatable data about what we do in the field of software engineering. There is much controversy about which data to collect, or even who should have access to it. Rules of thumb are the measures we use.

Scientists assume that the world really exists, and our senses tell us what it is like. We, in programming, probably cannot know the abstract world of information in the same way scientists know the concrete one. Even if we could, our senses aren't reliable sources of information about it.

So, while we are able to produce things of value, and have a solid track record of doing so, we run up against a limit that is inherent in all craft work: to learn what is technically possible from insight into nature. It is this insight that allows buildings with walls of glass to be possible and that convinces us we cannot fly without mechanical aid.

Without this insight, we must rely on procedures, just as the craft guilds did centuries ago. The effects are similar. We have become conservative, almost religious in our attitudes. We have arguments similar to those about how many angels can dance upon the head of a pin. We are pulled this way and that by those who have the knowledge of the Right Way and the True Faith. New doctrines appear, rise to prominence, and then recede. New standards are created and enforced without reality testing.

During the Age of Faith, cathedrals were built with high bell towers to help control demons. The church leaders assumed that evil spirits "can produce winds, storms, and rain of fire from heaven." [Seckel and Edwards 1986] Christian churches tried to ward off the bad effects of storms and lightning by ringing the bells to "temper the destruction of hail and cyclones and the force of tempests and lightning; check hostile thunders and great winds; and cast down the spirits of storms and the powers of the air." [ibid] This practice was based on a logically valid argument: that is, if demons caused the noise, then the noise of the sacred bells should affect them and bring them down.

Unfortunately, this practice also caused the electrocution of many bell ringers. In Germany, over a thirty-year period, 120 bell ringers were killed. [ibid] Bell ringing during storms continued in general use for many years, although some localities eventually prohibited it.

One might imagine the bell ringers trying to evade the dangers of the procedure while remaining loyal to the doctrine. Imagine the archbishop, who was the ultimate keeper of the True Faith, passing the responsibility for ringing the bells down to the auxiliary bishop, who transferred it to the monsignor, who passed it on to the pastor, who passed it to the priest, and priest to deacon, deacon to layman, who finally passed it off to Quasimodo. In a sense, those of us who labor under the doctrine of our field are all Quasimodos; struck by lightning while trying to protect the faith. (See Figure 1-1.)

Then, in the Age of Reason, Ben Franklin invented the lightning rod (1752). "One would think," he wrote, "it was now time to try some trick [to protecting churches and homes];—and ours is recommended." [ibid] His invention answered some important questions,

such as why would God allow lightning to strike innocent structures—like trees—or even worse, consecrated structures—like
churches. Something else was at work. Piety had nothing to do with
lightning strikes.

Figure 1-1. Protecting the Faith

Nevertheless, using lightning rods was seen by many to be
impious, and there was resistance to installing them. So, the danger
persisted. Eventually, science succeeded, and even though the
procedure for demon control remained in effect, it was in churches
equipped with lightning rods. (Although churches continued to be
built with steeples so demons would slide off the roof and could not
enter.)

The field of software engineering is in a transition between a kind of Age of Faith and an Age of Reason. We are not engineering yet, but we are getting there. Elements of the other sciences that examine our field might coalesce to provide the foundation for a central theory of our field. And, we do have some things going for us that might make up a proto-science.

Our field is essentially based on problem solving, which is closer to an *essence* about existence than most other sciences. While the others use problem solving to obtain information and theories about the world, they seldom reflect on the activity of problem solving itself. We, however, must look into the very *nature* of problem solving. We will face questions such as whether or not there really is order in the world, or whether such order is impressed upon it by our problem solving. And, does it make any difference either way?

Close at hand will be certain principles much like those in other sciences. Parsimony and Beauty are two that come to mind. "Keep it simple!" and "Make it look pretty!" are their equivalents in our field. Why are these principles so compelling? We might have to search for an answer. Coherence and Coupling could be looked at to see if they might not be a basis for theorizing about nature. When you examine them, you find they are both *sizing* rules. If your code doesn't cohere, then it is too large: better to break it up into smaller units. If your code operation depends on the operation of another module, then it is too small: better to make it big enough to include the other operation.

Why is it that modules that cohere functionally are *better* than those that do not? What is behind the idea that coupling is undesirable? It is mysterious. We know they are sensible rules, but we don't know *why*. "The key to the craft ... is to find rules. There is a classical discipline of computer science that embodies a couple of the major rules to be found, and your best programmers are aware of those several universal rules." [Lammers 1986, p.217]

It is apparent among us that we have a great desire to do our work. We often hear from others about how motivated we are. I have found this to be true. But, what lies behind this great desire? What is really going on here? Do we sense something beyond the obvious; is there something in the shadows? It is a wonderful mystery.

For now, the term "software engineering" is itself more a statement of our aspirations than the status of our field. We, as craftsmen, have already changed our world. As engineers, perhaps we can remake it.

CHAPTER TWO
A Personal View of the "State of the Art" in Programming

One way of looking at the context of programming is by examining how "close" we are to the machine. This is determined largely by the language we use. In close to the computer, we use machine or assembly languages, first- and second-generation languages respectively. As we move farther away, we use third-, fourth-, and soon fifth-generation languages. In close, we have complete control over the machine's capabilities. However, we give up some visibility of the problem to be solved because the machine "gets in our way." As we move further away, we begin to give up some control over the machine, but we gain visibility over the problems we are solving. The languages and our view become more abstract. (See Figure 2-1.)

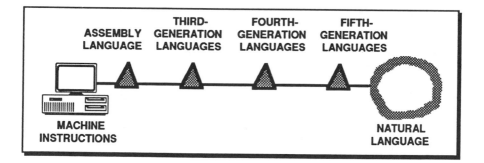

Figure 2-1. The Context of Programming

I suspect there is an optimal distance and, therefore, an optimal language for programmers trying to write applications, another language for the casual or end user, and still another language for systems and embedded-systems programmers.

A second continuum lies in a dimension that is at right angles to the first. It starts from input/output bound applications usually written in COBOL, such as transaction-based systems. It proceeds along to management information systems and decision support systems, which require more processing. It terminates at the process-bound applications found in engineering and scientific applications, which are so often written in FORTRAN. This continuum lies at some distance from the machine, appearing very clear at the distance of the third-generation languages. (See Figure 2-2.)

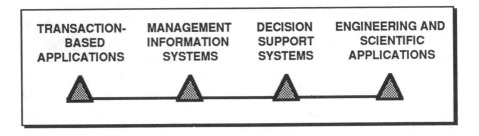

| TRANSACTION-BASED APPLICATIONS | MANAGEMENT INFORMATION SYSTEMS | DECISION SUPPORT SYSTEMS | ENGINEERING AND SCIENTIFIC APPLICATIONS |

Figure 2-2. An Application Continuum

There is something more here than just some cursory description of the differences between business and scientific applications.

Problems in the business realm tend to be rather arbitrary, unpredictable, and very, very large. The language COBOL is very verbose. It takes about five times as much COBOL to do the same work than when expressed in FORTRAN. And it isn't modular. Sure, it has paragraphs that can be written cohesively, but all the paragraphs in the same program module have access to all the information in the data division.

To make matters worse, it is common to assign a programmer the requirements for as many functions as can be designed and written in a specified period of time. This makes it tough to write coherent code. One of my correspondents says that writing COBOL is like living in a dormitory. Yet, the answers we have to produce in many cases have to be exact. My paycheck is delivered exactly to me, and not to me plus or minus one person. One of my teachers described a class of COBOL trainees as "a nervous group with anxious trembles and blank stares." That is the feeling I remember when I learned COBOL. It always seemed on the verge of chaos.

Engineering applications are ultimately a reflection of the *physics* of the problem and are much more regular and predictable. They aren't, or up until now haven't been, as large as the business monsters, and are often expressed in the mathematics of the problem. Mathematics is not only a language, but involves problem-solving techniques. Programmers using FORTRAN are already problem solvers in having brought with them their knowledge of mathematics. FORTRAN and the other languages used in the engineering field are very modular. And, more than that, they reflect Nature, which is determined. (If you understand the laws of nature, you understand both nature and that nature is not arbitrary.) One of my correspondents, remarking on languages with strong data types in scientific areas, commented, "Nature is already strongly typed. You can't add 1 to wind!" It has always seemed an orderly environment in which to work. Strangely, however, in engineering the answers are approximate with varying degrees of precision.

So far, we have two dimensions to look at: The distance from the machine or degree of abstraction, and a continuum from data-oriented to process-oriented problems.

Lying along the application continuum is one composed of organizational forms. At one end is the very large developer, such as a government agency. In such an environment, systems are developed in organizations called "programs" (not to be confused with computer programs). Programs are composed of a series of projects that can be done independently. The "program office" farms out the work to contractors who actually do the work. And the program office has an intense interest in costs and quality. Therefore, the project organizations themselves tend to be very large and complex to account for the cost and quality requirements of the large agency. (See Figure 2-3.)

Figure 2-4 shows a typical activity structure for a program. It is an illustration of the System Development Life Cycle from the Department of Defense (DoD). [DOD-STD-2167, 4 June 1985] Notice that it shows a "creeping commitment" by performing concept exploration and demonstration activities before full-scale implementation is attempted. This represents an ideal process compared to a real one in which politics play a role, affecting the initial steps in some projects.

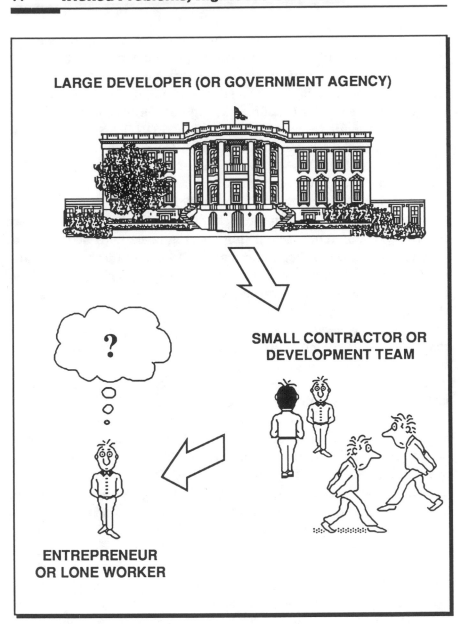

Figure 2-3. Types of Organizations

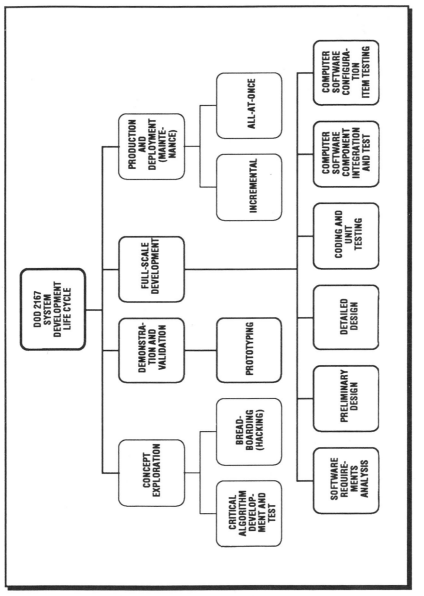

Figure 2-4. The DoD System Development Life Cycle

Another structure occurs in smaller institutions, such as corporations, which must often conform to government regulations when producing for the government, but which often take on a simpler form in the effort of pursuing their internal goals with computers. A typical chart for producing business systems is shown in Figure 2-5. Here, the main strategy is developed by high-level management. This is interpreted by middle-level managers into a series of projects that together will implement the main strategy. Each project takes on a life of its own and does the specific work to which it is assigned. Finally come the steps in the project itself.

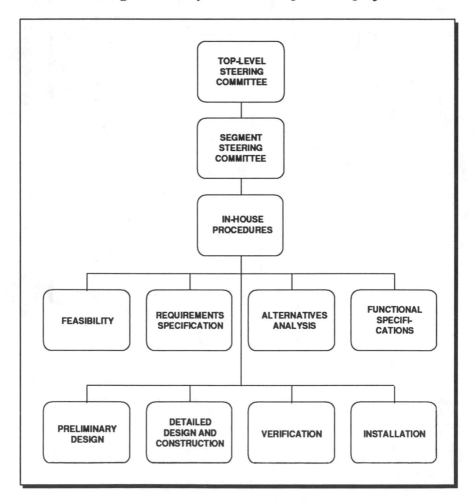

Figure 2-5. Business Systems

A continuing problem is integrating the activities of various projects, especially those undertaken in very large organizations. Some of the difficulties are: corporate activities that are geographically disbursed, communication services that are inadequate, and management structures that are too brittle.

An example of an engineering project is shown in Figure 2-6. This is similar to the DoD model, but simpler. There is a risk management aspect to it in that a problem solution is explored and demonstrated before full-scale production is attempted. Often, engineering applications are at the limits of technology and the risks of failure are higher. In business systems, developers customarily use a lower, more proven level of technology. Their problems occur in other areas.

Let's look again at Figures 2-4, 2-5, and 2-6. You will notice that there are many unusual terms included in them, such as hacking, prototyping, incremental, and all-at-once. We will talk about these in detail in Chapter Six, "Prototyping," and in Chapter Seven, "The All-At-Once Model."

At the far end of this spectrum is a single worker or a very small team producing applications for themselves or products to take to market. Here, initial deliberation often comes in the form of an inspiration—a great idea for a program. This illustration is even simpler, as shown in Figure 2-7. But, just because it is simple does not mean that it is ineffective. Such programs as dBASE, BASIC, PostScript, and Lotus 1-2-3 were produced by a single entrepreneur or small team.

The biggest advantage of the small producer is the degree of control over the project. Decisions are made and implemented rather quickly, and risk seems to be better managed. Most of these guys aren't betting the jobs of a lot of other people on a single product or decision. When they fail, we seldom hear about it and they go on to other things. Conversely, we certainly heard about Osborne and other computer companies failing during the shake outs that have occurred in the past few years.

So, the contexts that are important for us in the discussion of software engineering models have to do with how abstract our problem is, where it is on the data/process continuum, and what type of organizational structure there is. Figure 2-8 shows these in a simple, graphical form.

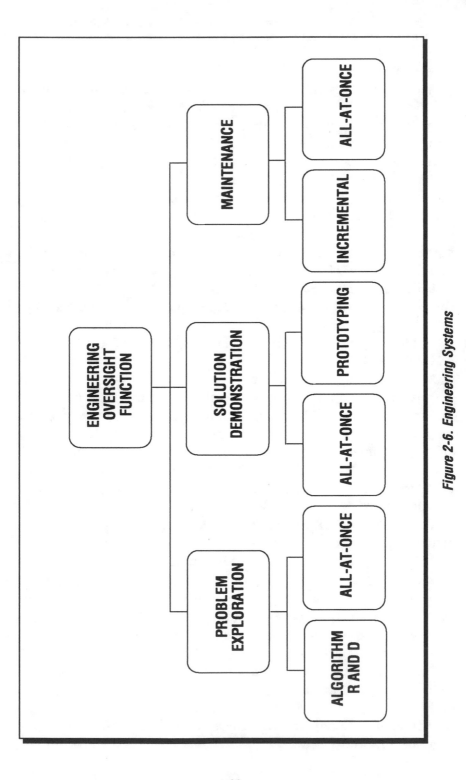

Figure 2-6. Engineering Systems

18

Figure 2-7. Entrepreneurial Inspiration

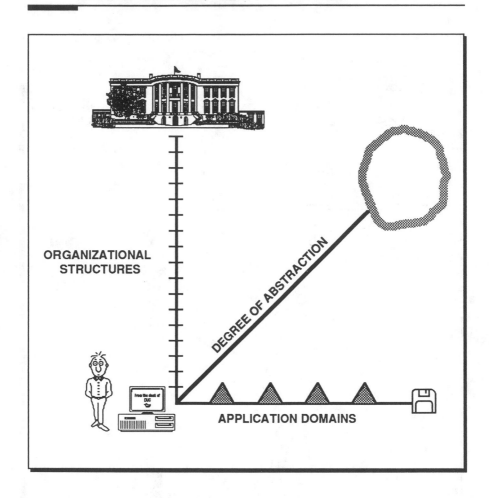

Figure 2-8. A Composite View

Somewhere near here is the territory of this book: the work models that we use. At first glance, it seems to map into the organizational continuum. It is similar, but where we are going is beneath the sociological viewpoint of how people group themselves, to perhaps a psychological description that describes what really goes on.

Fads, Fashions, and Who We Are

All of this is overlaid by our "reputation," which is not good and has given rise to the "software crisis." An exaggerated description of this crisis comes from a frequently cited report, GAO FGMSD-80-4, which is summarized in a footnote in IEEE Transactions in Software Engineering [SE-10, July 1984, p.38]. This report listed horror story after horror story:

50% of software contracts had cost overruns
60% had schedule overruns
45% of software could not be used
29% was never delivered
19% had to be reworked to be used
3% had to be modified to be used
Only 2% was usable as delivered

One would think that a study like that coming out of the Government Accounting Office really nailed us. Since then, great efforts have been made to "improve" us, and large markets have sprung up to serve this need.

But, as Blum points out, the study was seriously flawed. [Blum 1987] It was too small (only nine cases were actually studied), not all the data was published, part of the report was actually positive about the contracted software, and the study focussed on mostly "problem" cases. So, you can see how grossly exaggerated this report was. Think about it—most software works. Businesses operate okay, airplanes stay in the air (usually), supermarkets keep their shelves stocked, and my paycheck gets to me. We're not doing so badly. But, the crisis has been used as the rationale for the fads and fancies we experience all the time.

Some of them are: Ada and other high-order language advances, object-oriented programming, artificial intelligence, expert systems, automatic programming, graphical programming, program verification, CASE, and workstations. Fred Brooks considers these as candidates for the title of Silver Bullet. [Brooks 1987] To him, a Silver Bullet is the magical device that saves us from the monsters that our familiar software projects sometimes turn into, just as familiar people were sometimes transformed unexpectedly into werewolves and were laid to rest by silver bullets. But, he says, they are directed at the accidents of software engineering, not the essence of it, and, therefore, cannot have the productivity impact claimed for them. The real issues, he says, are complexity, conformity (and by this he means that software must bend to the arbitrariness of the human institutions and systems to which the software must provide an interface), changeability, and invisibility. To him, the real impact will come from buying versus building, prototyping, incremental development (grow—don't build software), and great designers.

Another writer seems to bear Brooks' notions out. Larry Peters wrote a paper entitled, *The "Chinese Lunch" Syndrome in Software Engineering Education: Causes and Remedies.* [Peters 1983] It appeared in an IEEE workshop on Software Engineering Technology Transfer, and he describes a common scenario in our field:

The decision makers in an organization perceive a need "to improve the way software is produced" (which is likely the effects of the "software crisis"). They decide to indoctrinate the technical staff in some new method or tool. (Few, if any, of the technical staff are involved in this decision.) The money is spent to acquire the method or tool and bring the organization up to date.

While some folks claim improvement, others complain that things have gotten much worse. "Before this new way of doing business was embarked upon, they could call on the technical staff and almost immediately some form of code was being developed. Bits and pieces were 'up and running'." [Peters 1983] Now they are being endlessly interviewed, and more often about issues that are more difficult to answer, such as issues about the future, etc.

These people begin to long for the good old days. Upper management notices that a great deal of money has been spent, but there is not a corresponding reduction in software development problems.

They conclude that the management involved is incompetent and should be replaced. The upgrading of training and technology ceases. A new management team is brought in, and the cycle repeats. "From a technology transfer standpoint, it is as though the organization had eaten some sort of 'Chinese Lunch' which left them wanting more within a relatively short period of time." [ibid]

Larry has taken some heat because of the title, and will probably take some more because of this reference. Some readers, I assume Chinese, resent the notion that their cuisine is not "filling." That is unfortunate. The Chinese restaurants in the area in which I work are always full during the lunch hour and, as far as I can tell, it is precisely because the food *won't* fill you up or bog you down.

Also, it *so* well describes the problem he presents. Are we not deluged by the Tool of the Week and the Method of the Month? Are not big promises made? And when upper management buys into the latest, how often does it pay off?

Larry goes on to list three causes. First, there is the "secret" (if we learn this secret, we will be successful) because there is one and only one way to solve the problem. If we are having problems, obviously, we aren't using THE way. It becomes a religious issue, not a technical one. Second, software engineering productivity (which seems to be the main problem complained about by upper management) is seen as a "technical" problem, and not a personnel or management problem. Therefore, it can be solved by buying a method or tool. And third, new tools and techniques can be had without really changing the life cycle in use. (I would prefer to say without requiring any real change on the part of managers and the people they manage.) He summarizes, "The latest in software engineering technology presents both a promise and a price. The promise is for better, easier to build, use and maintain software systems. The price is increased understanding and recognition of the human element in the software engineering equation ..." [ibid]

Both Brooks and Peters point back to us, the programmers, as key to positive change in software engineering. Another writer, Henry Ledgard [1987], has some pointers that might help achieve this change. They have to do with professionalism. He writes that most people think that the programmer population is divided neatly into amateurs and professionals. However, there is another class—

amateurs who are called professionals. He refers to them as P-sub-A (P_a) programmers. There are four types. First are the amateurs who think they are professional, such as recent graduates. Second are the amateurs who are learning to be professional, such as the journeymen who are transitioning to professional ranks. Third are the professionals who are really amateurs, such as those promoted for reasons other than for having the necessary skills. And fourth is the professional who does not reach out or has not taken the time to learn or keep up.

He goes on to describe nine characteristics of the P_a professional and the P_p programmer: An amateur assumes that the user is just like the programmer, while the pro never assumes user knowledge. An amateur sees anomalies as a way of life, while the pro's design includes "unusual cases." An amateur considers review a nuisance, while the pro welcomes it. The amateur is continually "trashing" out the bugs, while the pro releases programs with no known errors. Amateurs write the documentation last—pros first. The amateur works from very incomplete specifications—the pro has them in great detail. The amateur doesn't conform to the life cycle—the pro has well-defined phases and hard benchmarks. P_as get on with the job—pros work with a concern for future and larger systems. Amateurs write for the computer—professionals write for human beings.

Ledgard is getting at a quality here that marks professionals in other fields. There is always a lot more going on than slavish implementation of some initial request. A pro's work reflects standards about his training, his understanding and concern about the quality of his work, and the benefit of his client. This something extra is sometimes referred to as hermeneutics, a sensing of essences of the user and his environment. It is just this quality that Ledgard finds absent in P_as.

These qualities can be known about, studied, learned, and, most importantly, expected of professionals. "One would think," Franklin wrote, "it was now time to try some trick [to protecting churches and homes];—and ours is recommended." [Seckel and Edwards 1986]

Summary

We work at various distances from the machine with accompanying sensitivities to the problems at hand. We work in various problem domains, stressing data at one end and process on the other. And, we work in various-sized organizations that have implications for an individual's sense of risk and scope. On top of that is a perceived "software crisis" that has spawned a large market to "improve" us, while the real improvement that is needed, professionalism, goes unsatisfied.

Let us now look at the life cycle.

CHAPTER THREE
The Waterfall Model

The first model I'll discuss is the Waterfall, so called because the effort cascades down the main divisions of what many believe are the essential components of software development.

The Waterfall model is composed of an ordered set of phases. Developers begin at the first phase and proceed "down" the method to the succeeding phases, visiting each in turn. The "output" from one phase becomes the "input" to the next. Each succeeding phase can be seen as refining the statements of the previous one, sometimes transforming them into a different language or notation. A typical Waterfall model is shown in Figure 3-1.

"The Waterfall is largely consistent with the top-down, structured programming model introduced by Mills in 1971." [Boehm 1985, p.23] It was adapted, we are told, from proven hardware development methods. It appeared in 1970, but had forerunners as early as 1956. [ibid, p.22]

This model is used for developing software along the whole continuum of application types ranging from transaction-based information systems, such as automatic tellers in banks, to Aerospace-Defense-Engineering applications (ADE), such as attitude control software for spacecraft.

The Waterfall model has powerful, logical arguments going for it. Boehm argues that software development is decomposed into necessary subgoals, each of which is reached by the successful completion of one of the phases, and that the order of these subgoals is arranged to yield the greatest success. [Boehm 1981, pp.38-39]

The Waterfall also makes efficient use of people's talents by allowing for specialization in the work to be done. This specialization generally corresponds to the phases themselves. This results in horizontal integration, where a specialist applies his craft at some phase and then moves on to the same phase of another project. In

27

addition, this organization roughly corresponds to the workers' experience, with the most senior personnel (people with a combination of the greatest knowledge, experience, and skill) performing at the initial phases, junior personnel performing at later phases, and the most junior personnel performing the maintenance tasks.

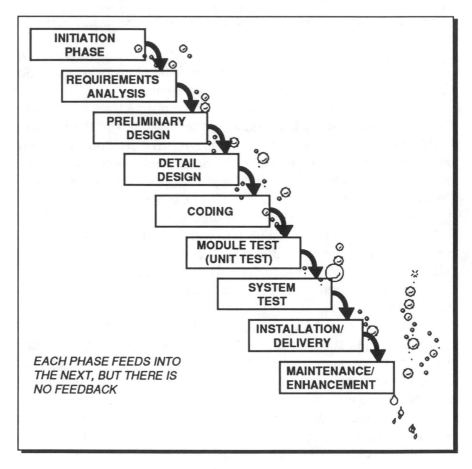

Figure 3-1. The Waterfall Model

The Waterfall model has strong appeal to management: It is orderly, it seems to be predictable (or at least it can be reported about), it facilitates the allocation of resources, and it meets or can be made to meet project and configuration-management requirements.

Briefly, the order is as follows: the first phase is usually called the Initiation Phase. It is followed by one or more phases for developing the software requirements and one or more phases for obtaining a software design. Then, there is a coding phase, a testing phase and, finally, phases for installation, maintenance/operations, and phase out.

There are many variations of the Waterfall, which makes it difficult to describe. In the following discussion, I will describe it from three different angles. First, I'll discuss the different starting and ending points. Then, I'll list the steps with the variations included. Finally, I'll discuss each step in detail.

Beginning and Ending Points

The Waterfall model has several beginning and ending points. It can start from initiatives by upper management, as in a business system (see Figure 3-2), or it can start from well within the system acquisition life cycle, as in engineering applications (see Figure 3-3).

Notice how the diagram of the business system suggests that a business project has a life of its own irrespective of other systems in the enterprise. Notice how an engineering project is frequently seen more in the context of its dependence on other engineering activities, such as technology assessment and the latest research and development, than does the business process. This is not always true, but it explains the independent flavor of business systems compared with engineering applications and with the later start of engineering projects.

There is another reason for the dependence of engineering software on other engineering activities. Much of the development of engineering software is *embedded* in major hardware components that were designed to perform only one set of tasks, such as an avionics system. Other types of engineering software executes on general-purpose computers. But, these general-purpose computers are *dedicated* to only one task, such as a computer that drives the dome of an astronomical observatory. The types of software that are embedded in the hardware or dedicated to only one task are very specialized, and are much closer to the machine, than are general-purpose business systems, where developers are isolated from the machine. The developers of engineering applications need to have a much closer relationship with the hardware and communications people than do the developers of business systems.

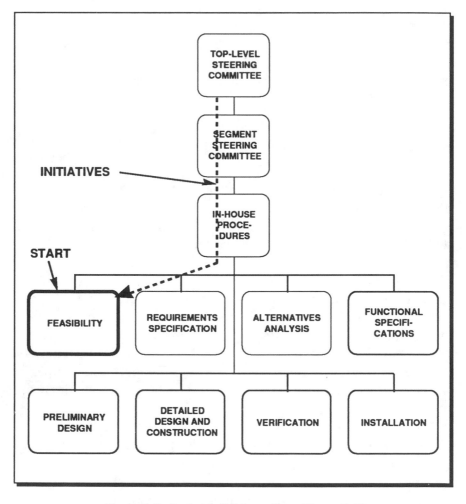

Figure 3-2. Business Systems (from Figure 2-5)

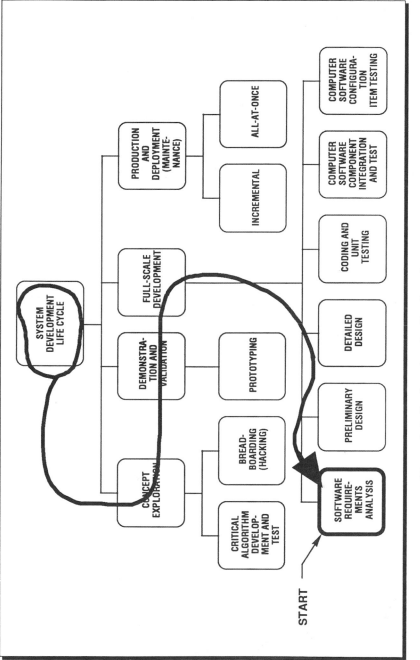

Figure 3-3. Engineering Applications (from Figure 2-4)

31

The ending points of these two types of systems can also vary significantly. In the business stream, development ends at the Installation phase. In the engineering stream, development ends earlier, at the Software Test phase, which is *before* system integration. Maintenance or Phaseout is the last step in either a business system or the more elaborate system acquisition life cycle. This last step then becomes the basis for the next Initiation step—something like the Hindu idea of repeating life cycles.

A great deal of attention has been paid to the initial phases of the life cycle, especially the Requirements and Design phases. The idea is that investing in these upstream activities will result in less downstream work and more reliable software. However, this idea is problematic. (See Chapter Four, "Problems With the Waterfall Model," and the subsection entitled "It Costs Too Much." If you are interested in doing some additional reading on this topic, there is some thoughtful work available: see *Research on Structured Programming: An Empiricist's Evaluation*, by Iris Vessey and Ron Weber in IEEE Transactions on Software Engineering, July, 1984. See also *Evaluating Software Engineering Technologies*, by David Card and others, in IEEE Transactions on Software Engineering, July, 1987. Neither of these works were able to show unequivocal support for such notions as top-down development or structured programming.)

Steps and Variations

The following are the traditional steps of the Waterfall with the variations I know about:

- Initiation (including an options study, which is sometimes a separate phase)

- Requirements Gathering and Analysis (including an alternatives study, which is sometimes a separate phase)

- Preliminary Design (including a functional specifications activity, which is sometimes a separate phase)

- Detail Design

- Coding (which is sometimes included in the Detail Design phase)

- Module Test (which is sometimes included in the Coding phase)

- System Test (verification)

- Installation and Delivery (validation)

- Maintenance and Operation (including a phaseout procedure, which is sometimes a separate phase)

As you can see, there can be as many as thirteen phases. Most Waterfalls use from six to nine phases, while some people admit to using only three.

Detailed Discussion

In describing each phase below, there are two streams to follow: (1) business and (2) Aerospace, Defense, and Engineering (ADE). Business and engineering problems have a lot in common; but, their approaches to the model vary, especially in the heavy "front-end" loading in business systems' software projects. We will look at each step in turn.

Initiation

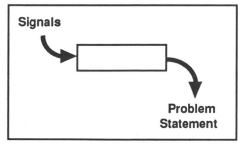

The Initiation phase is the beginning of a business application, whereas the Requirements Analysis phase, which is discussed just a little later, is usually the beginning of an engineering application.

The Initiation phase often originates at the senior management level, either as a result of strategic planning or arising from the operations of the business. (See Figure 3-2.)

The problem to be solved is stated in a general way, often as only an objective. Sometimes, management applies initial priorities and limitations, such as: "This project is of strategic importance, but is must be done for under five million dollars." My correspondents tell me that applying these initial priorities and limitations is useful later on when they are attempting to limit the project to a manageable size or keep it on track.

A team of people with the appropriate knowledge and skills is formed to evaluate the problem and propose solutions. Some interpreters of the theory conclude that there is no need here for assistance from computing experts. The bulk of the analysis is performed by the users, since they are most familiar with the problems they want to solve. However, as we shall see, this leads to problems.

The team uses the original problem statement, often in the form of a memorandum, an authorization to spend resources, and whatever documentation exists for the present system if there is one. The team then sets about expanding and clarifying the original statement, refining it for evaluation, and describing the problem in terms of the present system and *its* problems and limitations. This "present" system used to be a manual one, such as a system for making out paychecks, where you would fill out a timecard and take it to a bookkeeper who would write out a check for you. However, these days, this type of paycheck system is likely to be a first- or even second-generation computer system.

Sometimes, a business system contains flaws that cannot be solved by automation, such as turf, cultural, and political issues. These must be identified and dealt with either by fixing the current system or by declaring these other issues as limiting factors in the new system.

Turf issues are problems of conflicting charters and feelings of ownership. For example, during a period of decentralizing their computing services, a data-center technology staff may feel that they should set the standards for workstations, while newer organizations, mainly originating from using groups, may feel that it is *their* charter to do that activity.

Cultural issues involve the terminology being used, the environment in which the system will operate, issues about what to produce and how to produce it, and the organization's place in the enterprise. There is a business culture, an engineering culture, and a data-center culture, all of which have different terminology and environments, produce different things, and make competing claims on the enterprises' resources.

Political issues involve decisions that affect more than one organization, such as who decides what hardware and software will be "standard" throughout the entire enterprise. Political issues also involve decisions about which organization will have the ultimate responsibility for the project being considered.

All of these issues should be discovered and expressed so they can be accounted for in the development cycle. Otherwise, there is a risk of encoding these flaws into software that will later seem to be harder even than concrete.

Options Study (if there is one)

The next activity, which is sometimes a separate phase, is called the Options Study or Feasibility Analysis. During this activity, the developers imagine a range of solutions,

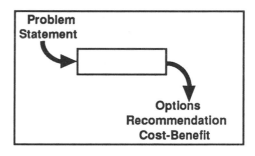

perform a cost-benefit analysis on each, apply any "spin" required by their own organization, pick the best candidate, and take it to their management for review and the authorization to continue. If approved, the information (a clarified, expanded problem statement, an Options Study, and a Cost-Benefit Analysis) is passed to the next phase for further analysis and refinement.

The Options Study provides management with a set of solutions to the problem they want solved. One of these options should always be: "Do nothing!" This allows management an "out": a cooling off period for the times when the "snake oil" salesmen come to town hyping the latest stuff your company should have.

Another reason to include a "do nothing" option is the "Abilene Paradox" first observed by Jerry Harvey [1988]. It goes something like this: One decision maker suggests a project, but has no good reason for it except to see what others will say about it. Well, as it often happens, the others have no real reason to object and they assume the suggester is highly motivated, so they go along with the suggested project. As a result, the project gets started and nobody really wants it.

A "Do nothing!" option allows decision makers a chance to reconsider and to escape the paradox early on, before a lot of money is spent on it. If you think this is hooey, please read Jerry B. Harvey, *The Abilene Paradox: The Management of Agreement*, Organizational Dynamics, Vol. 17, No. 1, Summer, 1988, pp.16-43.

Two documents are created during the Options Study, which are the deliverables for this phase: an options analysis and the preliminary cost-benefit analysis. The following are sample outlines for these documents:

- **Options Analysis Document—Contents**

  - Problem Definition
    - Problem statement (including a brief description of the enterprise)
    - Description of problems with current environment
    - Description of processes involved
    - Description of the organizations involved
    - Statement of the goals in solving the problem (if the problem goes away, what would things be like)

  - Potential Solutions
    - Assumptions and constraints (turf issues, etc.)
    - Potential solutions (repeat as necessary)
      — Descriptions
      — Impact of this solution on the organization
      — How this solution maps into the goals

  - Proposed System
    - Evaluations of all potential solutions
    - Recommendation and justification
    - Operational description of the proposed system

- **Preliminary Cost-Benefit Analysis Document**

  - Benefits
    - The goals that can be attained by this solution
    - Other benefits
      — Revenue improvements
      — Cost savings
      — Productivity improvements
      — Informational improvements
      — Other benefits

  - Costs
    - Development (labor and material)
    - Maintenance per year

  - Analysis
    - Net improvements
    - Net investment summary
    - Payback analysis
    - Cash-flow analysis

Requirements Gathering and Analysis Phase

In a business cycle, the inputs to this phase are the original problem statement and the options analysis and the cost-benefit analysis from the Initiation and Options Study steps. (See Figure 3-4.)

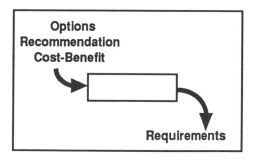

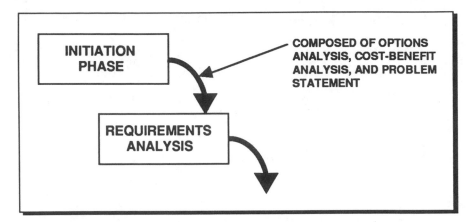

Figure 3-4. Inputs Flowing to the Requirements Phase in a Business Cycle

As I mentioned in the discussion of the Initiation phase, the Requirements phase is the beginning of the engineering software development life-cycle, which gets its inputs from system engineering activities. These inputs consist of a system specification, a design document for a segment of the system, a preliminary software requirements specification, an interface requirements specification, and a software development plan. (See Figure 3-5.)

Either of these sets of inputs, then, makes up the problem statement that is given to software developers.

During this phase, the software engineers develop a complete set of requirements. These requirements are the next step in refining the solution statement. If, for example, the solution statement includes using an information repository, the requirements might refine it to a type of database; if velocity is part of the answer, then the requirements would have the equation for calculating it.

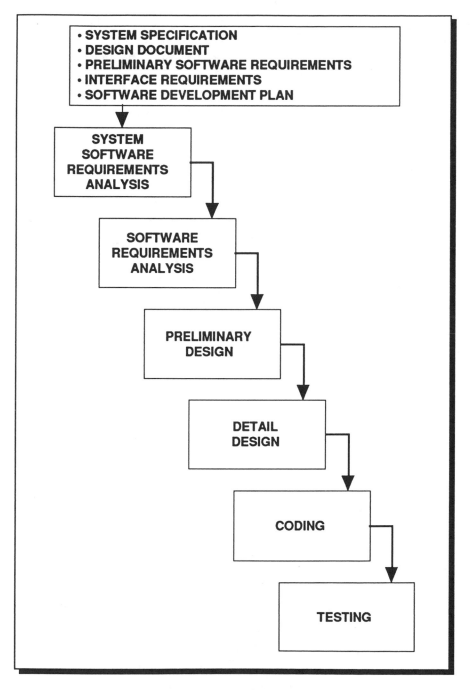

*Figure 3-5. Inputs Flowing to the Requirements Phase from
System Engineering Activities*

In a typical business project, the organization that is expected to use the new system assigns a program manager who, in turn, acquires and trains the development team. The team members review the project documentation to date, prepare a statement of work and task breakdown structure, and obtain the necessary approvals. They then put in place planning, control, and reporting mechanisms and publish preliminary schedules. They also identify the organizations and processes that are affected by the project.

Once the team has made these initial preparations, they carefully analyze the existing system. They interview users and collect the forms, reports, and procedures that were previously identified. They use this information to determine the data processes that occur in each of the using organizations. They note the specific problems and concerns of those in the using organizations. Also, at this stage, the constraints of the Initiation phase are first applied to weed out unnecessary requirements and control the size of the Preliminary Design phase downstream.

Finally, the developers collect any new business requirements that improve or correct the current system and identify the areas of impact on the user and any changes to organizations.

The development team analyzes all the material collected so far and then invents a new system. This is the creative part of the process. Notice how much time is spent here on talking and reporting about the job, and how little time is spent on actually doing the job. This is common in all of the Waterfall models I examined.

These procedures seem to be very simple and straightforward, but they have very little to say about exactly how the new system is invented. Is it really as simple as it sounds?

In engineering applications, the project preparations, such as choosing the project manager, assembling the project team, and developing the organization, occurred during the previous phase. However, similar architectural activities occur during the Requirements phase. The processing aspects of computing—algorithms, equations, various parameters for scaling, and other sizing tasks—are determined. And, some capacity measurements are made on the target computer.

For either stream, popular notations such as Data Flow Diagrams (DFDs), Entity Relationship Diagrams (ERDs), and Hierarchical Input Process Output Diagrams (HIPO charts) are used.

So, in reality, this is probably the most difficult phase to get right. There is a lot of interaction between the technical people and the customers. There is some flux about the problem and its solution. And, this step includes a significant paragraph that I have found in one form or another in most of the various Waterfalls I have examined: The recommended solution is *descriptive* in nature. That is, the proposed system is described in terms of *what* it must do for the users. At this stage, no attention is yet paid to *how* it will work. That will be done in the next step—Preliminary Design.

There have always been problems with the concept of describing all of the "whats" in the Requirements step and all of the "hows" in the Preliminary Design step. Often, the steps are intermixed. This is sometimes attributed to a lack of training or experience on the part of the developers. However, I suspect it because breaking the "whats" and "hows" into separate steps is an unnatural way of working. I will have more to say about this later.

Several other complications arise in this phase. A very large system, like an airline reservation system, often cannot be brought up at one time and must be phased in. If this is so, then planning for that phasing begins here. Also, by this time the project has become large enough to take on a life of its own, with all the interaction and reporting that implies. If subcontractors or vendors are going to be involved in the project, those activities begin here. These include the initial contacts with vendors and subcontractors; forming contracts with them and other implied legal matters; offsets from international purchases, minority enterprises, etc.; and then continuing the contacts with the vendors and subcontractors.

Alternatives Study (if there is one)

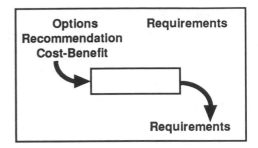

The Alternatives activity that occurs in this phase (or sometimes in a separate, succeeding phase) creates another complication. The system architecture is determined here, along with several alternatives among the variations that exist in the main solution, which was selected earlier. This is not to be confused with the Options Study performed in the Initiation phase. There, we were concerned with selecting one out of several solutions. Here, we are concerned with selecting from among the variations *within* the solution.

Think of it this way. After deciding to solve your transportation problem by getting a car (one solution chosen from several options), you must now decide what *type* of car—new or used; silver, blue, or red; and compact, mid-size, or full-size (the varying alternatives within the solution).

Often, the Alternatives activity is deleted because the questions that are usually asked in this phase have already been answered, such as what hardware, telecommunications, and other resources would be used. This is especially so in applications shops doing mainframe MIS or engineering applications, and less so in embedded systems shops and in PC applications because of the rapid changes taking place.

If the Alternatives Study is performed here, the typical deliverables from it are the following documents: a requirements document, a preliminary program plan and, sometimes, an alternatives analysis report. The following are sample outlines for these documents:

- **Requirements Document**
  - Boilerplate
  - Project scope
  - Project history to this point
  - Current system description (DFDs, ERDs, HIPO charts)
  - New system description (DFDs, ERDs, HIPO charts)
  - New system requirements (DFDs, ERDs, HIPO charts)

- **Preliminary Program Plan**
  - Statement of work
  - Work breakdown structure
  - Management plan
  - Documentation plan
  - Visibility and tracking plan
  - Schedules

- **Alternatives Analysis Document**
  - Objective
  - Scope
  - Operational approach
    - ❏ alternative 1
    - ❏ alternative 2
    - ❏ alternative n
  - Technical approach
    - ❏ approach 1
    - ❏ approach 2
    - ❏ approach n
  - Recommendation

After the Alternatives Study is complete, the options and cost/benefits plans are updated, another review and approval activity is undertaken, and all of this material is fed to the next phase: Preliminary Design.

Preliminary Design Phase

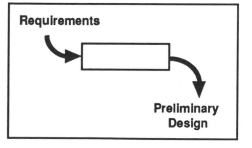

The Preliminary Design phase is sometimes divided into two phases: Functional Specifications and Preliminary Design. The dogma about when or whether this split into two phases occurs isn't always explicit, but it has to do with whether or not you are strictly interpreting structured analysis (that is, you have an old physical and an old logical, and a new physical and a new logical description of the system). Some other contributing factors are the size, culture, and makeup of the project, and the state of the current doctrine.

Business systems often have a Functional Specifications phase in which the user's view of the new system is designed, reviewed, and approved. When it is acceptable, the new system is designed down to the modular level in the Preliminary Design phase.

Functional specifications provide a bridge between the "whats" of the requirements analysis and the "hows" of preliminary design. Some of the program's architecture is determined here, along with screen and report layouts. Menus are also determined here. But, users still play a significant role in verifying that their needs will be satisfied. The system is described as completely as possible in the users' language and in the users' view. Software, hardware, and other features that will *appear* to the users are shown. All inputs, outputs, and transformation rules are defined. The operating environment, the hardware and software environment, the constraints of the system, and allowances for future contingencies are shown. These functional specifications are the last opportunity for the users to respond before the system is produced.

In typical engineering applications, a user's view is not necessary and the Waterfall goes from the Requirements Analysis phase to the Preliminary Design phase without any intermediate steps.

In the Preliminary Design phase, all the information from requirements and functional specifications is merged to arrive at the system architecture, which is typically displayed in a structure chart.

The partitioning of the system into various modules is an art. It is seldom a one-to-one mapping of the data flow diagrams from the previous steps into a structure chart. The designer's task is to arrange the functions in an order that is both efficient and economical of computer resources. The designer may, for example, arrange all the functions that take input from outside the program into one module or a set of modules, but might not do this for functions that deliver output from the program. Instead, the developer may want to isolate all processing from any I/O operation, but may also distribute some processing among I/O modules to determine and correct errors and build up a complete entry before processing it.

The Preliminary Design phase typically produces the following documents as its deliverables:

- **Functional Specification Document**
  - System overview
  - Detailed functional flow (context diagrams)
  - Detail process specifications
  - Logical data model

- **Preliminary Design Document**
  - Introduction
  - System architecture
  - System structure
  - Subsystem design
  - Preliminary database design
  - Production/test environments
  - Module design
  - Implementation plan
  - Hardware requirements

- **Updated Program Plan**

- **Final Cost-Benefit Analysis Document**

- **Resource Estimates and Schedules through Completion of the Program**

- **User Test Plan**

- **User Training Plan**

- **Test Plan Outlines**

- **Conversion Requirements**

- **Estimate of Resources Required for the Next Phase**

Detail Design Phase

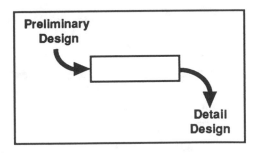

In this phase, the modules are designed using information provided by structure charts and other diagrams produced in the previous phases. The Detail Design phase varies significantly between the business and ADE streams. In the business stream, Detail Design is combined with the Coding and Module Test phases. The description that follows is from the business stream, but has analogs in engineering in this and later steps.

Detail Design and Construction: The modules defined in the Preliminary Design phase are completely designed in this step. Program Design Languages (PDLs), which made an appearance in earlier phases, and the third-generation language chosen for implementation in the Requirements phase, are used here.

The function that each module must perform is written in a PDL (structured English) or a high-order language (such as Ada). Ordinarily, it cannot be compiled, but sometimes it can be transformed into graphic representations. Sometimes, it is even compiled in an early attempt to detect design flaws.

Upon completion of the program design, the designer conducts a review with peer designers of the just-completed design. He creates support software that should include the following items: Version control (to permit one version of a program or system to be used as the baseline for the next); automatic listing of the contents of the current library; housekeeping procedures to allocate, catalog, restructure, and maintain the libraries; recovery procedures to provide backup and recovery of the libraries; and previously written job control language sets for specific processes.

Each module is transformed into portions of a computer program that can be compiled individually or assembled into larger units that will then be compiled. Sometimes, the procedure portion of the program can be created by generating statements in the target language directly from the structure charts. Input and output descriptions, such as the screen formats, report formats, and record/segment formats, are generated using various utility programs and are defined in the data definition portion of the program. The code is compiled and syntax errors are corrected. "Smart" compilers also provide information that is useful during testing.

Following the coding and compilation, a walkthrough is conducted to demonstrate that the code conforms to the design, which is another way of saying "looking for errors." When that is completed, the unit testing of the module is conducted.

Developers next prepare for converting data to the new system. Some of the data might already exist, some of it will be converted from one electronic form to another or from hardcopy to electronic form, and some of it will be newly generated and collected.

Additional data might be added from separate sources; created during the operation of the system; only applied to new records and not retroactively applied to existing records; or converted from files that exist as separate files into an integrated database.

Then, the developers complete the system user's manual. This manual must convey all the information that is necessary for the user to understand the system, to prepare all types of input, to interpret output, to understand how the output was derived, and to use the system efficiently and thoroughly with little or no assistance.

And last, but certainly not least, the developers prepare the programmer's manual. This is one of the key items for maintenance programmers. It contains a context diagram, descriptions of the files used by the system, and a readable copy of the data dictionary, if there is one. It has references to all the other documents produced so far, and might even contain some of the requirements and design information.

The following list is a summary of the tasks that might be performed during the Detail Design phase. Their next phase is System Test (Verification). However, engineering software developers have separate Coding and Module Test phases. As you can see from this list, detailed design is a very busy time for the developers of business systems. It is so busy that many of the tasks are given short shrift or overlooked altogether. In addition, if the technical writers have not been involved up until now, much of the documentation suffers the same fate: the user's manual is incomplete and the programmer's manual is nonexistent.

Task List:

- Create the program structure charts
- Define the test plan
- Define the input and output data
- Conduct the design review
- Develop the JCL support library
- Set up the developmental and test support libraries
- Translate the module design to code
- Generate screen definitions
- Prepare the module test data
- Compile the module source code
- Conduct the module walkthrough
- Conduct the module unit test
- Add the module to the support library
- Demonstrate and turn over the module to the customer
- Review the database design
- Determine the source for each data element
- Prepare a specification defining how each data element will be provided for the database
- Define the general system flow
- Define any unique terms
- Define the input data and formats
- Define the output data and formats
- Explain diagnostic messages
- Define corrective actions
- Describe how to get assistance

Deliverables:

- System modules ready for user test
- Conversion specifications
- System user's manual
- Programmer's manual

Coding Phase

With the Coding phase, we are returning to discussing the phases in the engineering stream. This phase and the Module Test phase are included in the business approach.

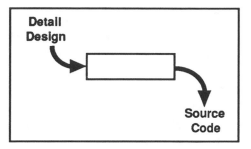

During this phase, the modules are coded. Sometimes, this activity is combined with the previous phase, and sometimes with the next phase.

Also during this phase, powerful optimizing compilers and the extensive use of libraries of both source and object code provide invaluable information for downstream activities.

Unfortunately, writing code is often seen as trivial, as if all the important work has already been done. But, this is the phase that produces all the pieces of the system.

Module Test Phase

In this phase, the modules are tested. Again, this phase is sometimes combined with the previous phase, and sometimes with the next phase.

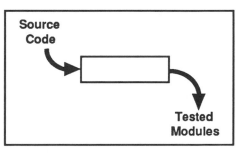

System Test (Verification) Phase

In the System Test phase, the modules are integrated into the new system. This phase also answers the question: "Did we build the system right?"

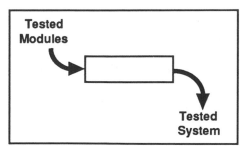

The operational deliverables and associated documentation created during the Detail Design and Construction phase are tested for (1) compliance with the functional specifications, and (2) compliance with the requirements document. The testing is performed by operating the hardware and software using test cases that were constructed to demonstrate compliance. Some of these test cases were developed or suggested in phases as early as Initiation. Figure 3-6 shows the relationships between various testing activities and the phase that each activity is verifying.

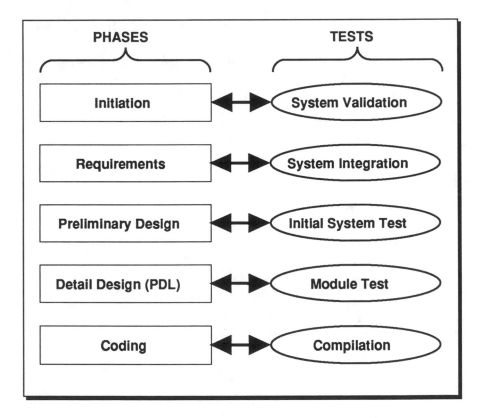

Figure 3-6. The Relationships Between the Phases and Tests

The deliverables for the System Test (Verification) phase are the following:

- **Test reports**
- **Training material**

Installation and Delivery (Validation) Phase

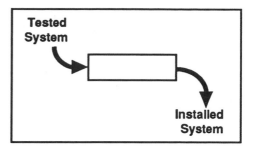

In this phase, the new system is installed and delivered to the users for acceptance testing. It answers the question: "Did we build the right system?"

The accepted system is installed into the production environment according to the implementation phasing plan defined in the Preliminary Design phase.

The installation involves data conversion, audit, and the implementation of data center operating procedures. The installation may span years, and ends when the user accepts all the phases of the system implementation plan.

All of this testing is a way of mapping what was synthesized into what was analyzed. The program is first mapped into the source code at compilation, into PDL at module test, into the preliminary design at initial system test, into the requirements at system verification test, and into the problem statement at validation and acceptance test. (See Figure 3-6.)

The deliverables during this phase are the following:

- **Installation plan**
- **Installed system**

Maintenance and Enhancement Phase

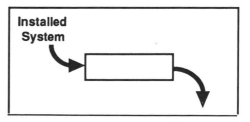

This phase usually begins with locating and fixing discrepancies and bugs. But, there are other things that go on in Maintenance. In fact, all of the activities of the Waterfall also go on in the Maintenance phase.

Maintenance programmers are almost always new to the system, and they must analyze the existing code to find out what it is doing. The documentation is almost always inadequate because of the crush of documentation and the tightening of schedules as the Waterfall progresses. So, the maintenance programmers are left with the source code as their main source of information about the system This helps in locating discrepancies between what the customer said they wanted and what they actually got.

For example, a very common discrepancy is that often the last line of reports does not print properly or does not print at all. This is commonly caused by setting your printer up with its line count off by one. The maintenance programmer must examine the code to try and determine where the error occurred.

The maintenance programmer also collects new requirements for later enhancements, and does some preliminary design, detailed design, and coding.

The bug-fixing activity usually begins by locating and fixing errors occurring at the highest rate the system will experience. The Mean Time Between Failures (MTBF) falls off quickly (one hopes) to be replaced by enhancement, which is extended development. The lower failure rate and on-going development continue for the life of large, mainframe systems, which is generally 10 to 15 years.

It is commonly understood that most of the cost of the system is in the Maintenance/Enhancement phase. It is also thought that the money spent up front will be recouped in lower maintenance costs.

Toward the end of this phase, or the phaseout step, agitation for a new system begins. The current system, which is now old and obsolete, becomes the target for a new problem statement, somewhat vaguely and generally described by upper management or a government agency, and the process is ready to begin all over again.

Old systems are often run against new replacement systems as a validation check. When the switch over comes, it is often phased so that the old system is not removed completely, but over a period of time.

But, many systems live on way beyond what one would expect in large organizations. While newer systems are installed and used by most of the organization, these old systems have somehow found a protected niche where they are well cared for and used as required.

Yet, they are not part of the mainstream, becoming a rivulet—a backwater—some quiet place where only a few people go. This is as it should be. As long as the system is still usable, why abandon it? Of course, there might come a time when it will cost more than it is worth, and will be terminated.

Closing Thoughts

In this closing, I have something to say about the importance of some of the parts of the Waterfall, such as the documentation, reviews, and the use of language.

Documentation

I have included brief outlines of the documentation produced in the phases of the Waterfall because, besides the software itself, the most important product of the Waterfall is documentation. It is more important than the graphing techniques, the analysis method, or the programming language used.

There are many adequate technical practices and languages, but there are only a few notions of documentation. There is good documentation, many gradations of bad documentation, and missing documentation.

Also, documentation is more important in software development than in hardware development. This is so because what we produce is invisible. Users, customers, and other outside parties (such as the dreaded auditors) have nothing concrete to go on in the early stages; project management needs something to judge the progress of the job; the developers up and down the line need good information to enable them to figure out what must be done next; and horizontal integration requires specialists to leave accurate complete records for the next guy in the process.

Verbal descriptions that are not stored permanently just won't do. But, many of my correspondents report that while their projects start off with good intentions, in an environment as formal as the Waterfall, software is often developed by word of mouth. Some of them complain that there is simply not adequate time allotted for documentation.

Within a project, there are several key points at which good documentation is more important than usual. The most important is the pass off from development to maintenance. This is not only the winding up of the development portion of the life cycle, but also the time where the next guy in line traditionally starts off knowing nothing about what he is to maintain.

As we have seen, maintenance is not only a time for fixing bugs (and you need a lot of good information to do it well), but it is also the time of extended development. It is very important to have a sense of what the users and developers had in mind when they did the project. It will lead you "beside the still waters" rather than through "the valley of the shadow of death." [King David, Psalms 23, The Bible]

A second point at which good documentation is important is the transition between analysis and design. This has always served as a summing up point for user inputs and requirements. And, a third point is between construction and test/integration. This is the verification time, and the documentation helps you to know what you are verifying the software against.

At any of these key points, flaws in the documentation cause grievous problems for the folks who are trying to use the documents to do their jobs.

Here is a list of all the documents that would be produced in the Waterfall:

- Original Problem Statement
- Options Analysis Document
- Cost-Benefit Analysis Document
- Requirements Document
- Preliminary Program Plan (which could have a lot of stuff in it)
  - Statement of Work
  - Work Breakdown Structure
  - Management Plan
  - Documentation Plan
  - Visibility and Tracking Plan
  - Schedules

- Alternatives Analysis Document
- Functional Specification Document
- Preliminary Design Document
- User's Guide
- Programmer's Guide
- User Test Plan
- User Training Plan
- Test Plan Outlines
- Test Reports
- Installation Plan

Not to mention the software itself, and all the associated software such as support libraries, job control language, configuration control programs, etc.

Here is what the Department of Defense wants in the way of documentation (from DOD-STD-2167A):

- Preliminary System Specification
- System Specification
- System/Segment Design Document
- Preliminary Software Requirements Specification
- Preliminary Interface Requirements Specification
- Software Development Plan
- Software Requirements Specification
- Interface Requirements Specification
- Software Design Document (Preliminary Design)
- Software Test Plan
- Preliminary Interface Design Document
- Software Design Document (Detailed Design)
- Software Test Descriptions
- Interface Design Document (Detailed Design)
- Source Code Listings
- Software Test Descriptions (Procedures)
- Software Test Reports
- Operation and Support Documents (there could be lots of these)
- Version Description Document
- Software Product Specification

Add to this seven reviews and audits, and the paperwork required for project management and configuration control, and you have a lot of hardcopy. And, all this is just to support the need for information about the software.

Conveniently, the 2167 standard offers templates for all of these documents. They are called Data Item Descriptions, DIDs in DoD parlance.

In addition, NASA has an even larger set of templates for documents. They are part of the Software Management and Assurance Program, known as SMAP by aficionados. IEEE also has several document standards that may be obtained through the American National Standards Institute (ANSI).

Reviews

The reviews conducted during the Waterfall process are its third most important, and usually most neglected, product. They provide us with very important information during the project and very useful information afterwards. They are a common artifact of engineering disciplines: engineers are expected to hold or participate in them as a part of maintaining their professional standing.

In the business stream of the Waterfall, the first review is really the Options Study, which gives management a time to reflect on whether this project is the best use of the Company's resources. The next review is the Alternatives Study, which is very useful in determining which kind of solution is best for the stated purposes. The famous "make or buy" decision is made here. (In the engineering stream, there are comparable review points.)

The functional specification of the Preliminary Design phase is another opportunity for a review, giving the customer a final say in what is to be developed. Finally come the design and code reviews of the Detail Design and Coding phases.

There are some problems with reviews. First, they are often politicized, becoming more like ceremonies than times of learning and reflection. Second, we all have blind spots and reviews can show us where they are. But, it is not readily accepted that blind spots are human and natural. They are too often seen as flaws to be kept hidden. As a result, reviews are often not done, are done in intimidating fashions, or are done with the results kept hidden.

One of the documents from the Waterfall should be a "lessons learned" report listing the reviews and how they affected the project.

A Word About Language

Language is used in many different ways in the Waterfall model. English is seen in several forms: informal, business, formal, and structured. Structured English is seen in problem statement languages (PSAs) and Program Design languages (PDLs). (See Figure 3-7.)

This is the side of the process that human beings can understand. After the compilers get the source code written in a programming language, it is transformed into a language that the machine can understand.

All of this activity—the Waterfall and the ways in which we use language—is in the service of transforming an initial need at initiation into a final product at testing. There are some interesting things about this transformation process.

First, there is the bilingual nature of many phases of the Waterfall, where an input could be stated in English and the output in a PDL. Yet, they are equivalent.

Second, the input to a process tends to be *less complex* than the output. The input is shorter, for one thing, and is usually expressed in terms that are more easily understood than the output.

Third, and strangely, any one item of *output* is *less* complex than the *input*, although taken as a whole this is not so. It is odd that as we decompose a process into its simpler components, we are adding to the complexity of the work as a whole.

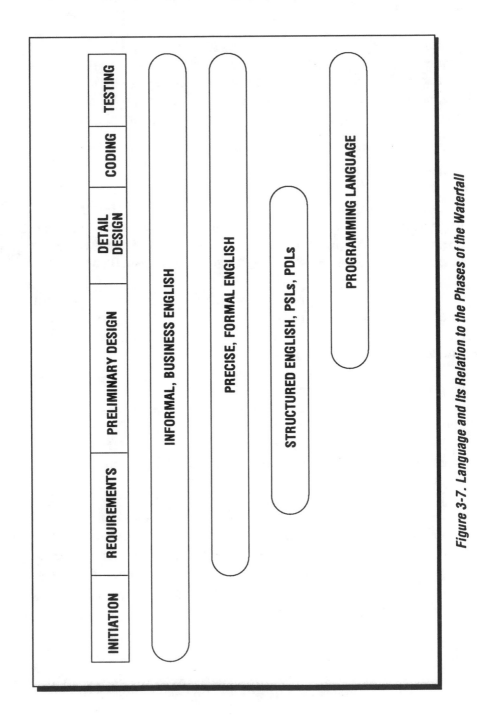

Figure 3-7. Language and Its Relation to the Phases of the Waterfall

Fourth, each transformation becomes a step removed from the origin or the user and a step closer to the final product. As we move farther away from the user at the origin, language becomes more and more abstract and we become more objective about it. We also tend to see the users and consumers of software objectively, almost as if *we* are not users and consumers of software ourselves. As we move closer to the final product, we are attracted to its emergence from the mists. In the early stages of a project, developers talk mostly to other folks; in the later stages, they talk mostly with machines.

Other technologies have scientists to abstract the world into principles about nature, and engineers who combine these principles together to make things useful and concrete. And, they usually have bits of hardware laying around to show that they have accomplished something. But, for us, we do all of it through language. We become Merlins, spinning out great and wonderful things from our incantations and spells.

Summary

I have not attempted an exhaustive description of the Waterfall, since many books have been written about it and many procedures such as DoD 2167 describe it in great detail. What I have attempted to do is to describe it well enough to provide information that will be useful for comparison with the models yet to come.

There are several things you should keep in mind about the Waterfall model. First, it is a formal method. By this I mean it is an orderly, systematic method of developing software. Second, it is a type of top-down development, closely related to structured analysis and design. Third, it is composed of phases that are seen as independent and are expected to be done in a strict sequence. Fourth, there is some variation in how it is used: sometimes steps are combined, and often there are different starting and ending points.

Finally, the Waterfall is part of a much larger cycle. Some call it a product cycle, others call it a marketing cycle. But, what it looks like is shown in Figure 3-8.

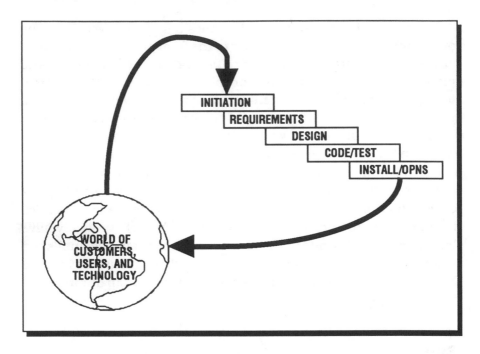

Figure 3-8. The Waterfall as Part of a Larger Cycle

The Initiation phase has received its input from signals from the marketplace, internal users, and technology. These signals are expressed in terms of profit and loss statements, suggestions and complaints, and reports about emerging technology and are used by the project's initiators to set the Waterfall in motion.

When the Waterfall is done, a product is returned to the signal makers who use it to adjust their messages.

Technology is a very interesting case, since computer programs are used as great information levers enabling scientists and engineers to have a new or clearer picture of their part of the world or product. The result is enabling technology, which, as it is reported to us, becomes a signal in itself.

We have now examined the famous Waterfall model for software engineering. It is a complex, stately process something like a queen's barge floating down the Nile. It is the model most talked about; the one most large organizations use to produce software. It is one way to manage the complexity and size of projects. But, it has some problems, and we will take a look at them in the next chapter.

CHAPTER FOUR
Problems With the Waterfall Model

As we have seen, the Waterfall is the most popular model and has strong arguments in its favor. As we shall see, many variants have been developed to take into account application domains and changing conditions. And, it can be tailored to meet application demands. Nevertheless, there are problems with it—some big, some little—some concern the model itself, and others concern things outside the Waterfall. Let us talk about those outside things first.

Some people argue that the Waterfall is not a development method at all, but rather a project-management technique. They bring as evidence the lack of actual techniques for producing software. I have analyzed several Waterfall descriptions and found more than 90% of the content devoted to talking and reporting about the job, while the remaining 10% describes what is to be done or how to do it. So, it would seem they have a point.

Nevertheless, it is expected that the software *will* be developed according to the model. NASA, the DoD, and many private firms insist on this. And, if the actual *methods* for production are absent, it is only because there are so many methods available and it is expected that users will plug in the methods they are using at the time. Besides, the notions of structured analysis and design are closely related to the Waterfall, and their use could understandably be assumed.

Structured analysis and design and the Waterfall model were introduced at about the same time as replacements for the code-and-go shops that were prevalent at the time they were developed. They fit together so well because the separate phases of requirements, two design phases, and the coding phase in the traditional Waterfall map so well to structured analysis, design, and programming (SADP), respectively. And, the outputs from these phases are often expressed in data flow diagrams, structure charts, and structured programming constructs.

I often use the term "formal methods" as a short-hand term meaning the Waterfall model combined with SADP. This is consistent with the experience of many organizations moving from the code-and-go shops and the views of many observers.

This is not to say that the Waterfall and SADP are only seen in terms of each other. But, frequently and typically, this is so. (See Figure 4-1.)

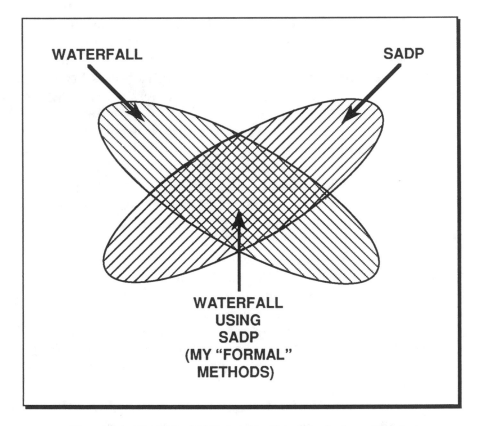

Figure 4-1. The Waterfall Using Structured Analysis and Design

Together, the Waterfall and SADP provide a formal method for development. But, there are problems with formal methods. Ordinarily, a formal method is a systematic, orderly way of doing something. But, there are other meanings given to the term "formal." It could mean, for example, concentrating on external appearance or form rather than substance.

Folks complain about the stacks of documentation that nobody (except a lawyer, perhaps) reads, but v h.ich, nevertheless, have to be produced. They complain about having to create and maintain current and new physical and logical models of the system. They find it tiresome to draw all those data flow diagrams and other graphs and then redraw them frequently. They feel they are doing it "for show—not know."

Formal methods, depending on how they are enforced, make it more difficult to take advantage of opportunities for improvement that may come along, either by restraining exploration or by constraining it to a small part of one phase.

Another problem with formal methods is the user's view of software development. Our Waterfall method is not "real" to them. If you are building a house, you soon notice the effects of your decisions on the phases of the construction: the lot you chose, the position of the house on the lot, preparing the land, pouring the foundation, etc. And, as each new event occurs, it becomes obvious to the builder that it is harder and harder to change his mind or correct mistakes. But, software is invisible and immaterial in the same sense that literature is immaterial. Users and customers of software have no intermediate events that "cast things in concrete" and, therefore, tend to change their minds often and at the most awkward times.

Here is an example of something cast in concrete that is hard to change. Suppose you are building a square house that is fifty feet on a side. (See Figure 4-2a.) You make a mistake when laying out the foundation. As a result, one corner projects one foot longer than the other corners. This means that *two* adjacent sides will be too long. (See Figure 4-2b.)

You discover the mistake *after* you have poured the foundation and it is already set. If the error is not corrected and the house is framed according to the foundation's shape, then none of the rooms on three of the outside corners will be square.

This has many implications for the rest of the construction, especially for the finishers such as the cabinet makers. In order to correct the mistake, you have to repour the two offending sides. This could done by widening the foundation walls on a taper from the offending corner, or by removing the two offending sides and setting new forms. Obviously, this is not easy.

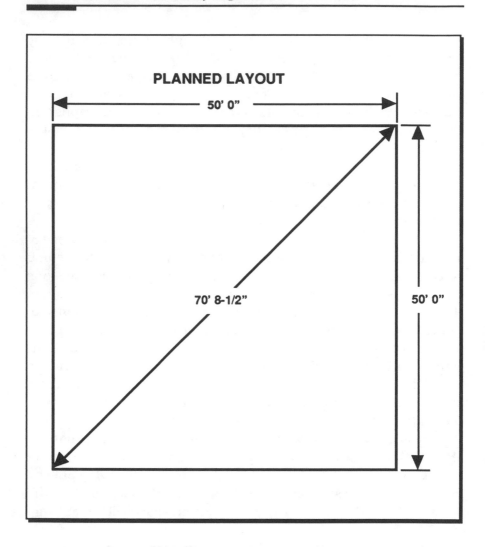

Figure 4-2a. The Planned Foundation

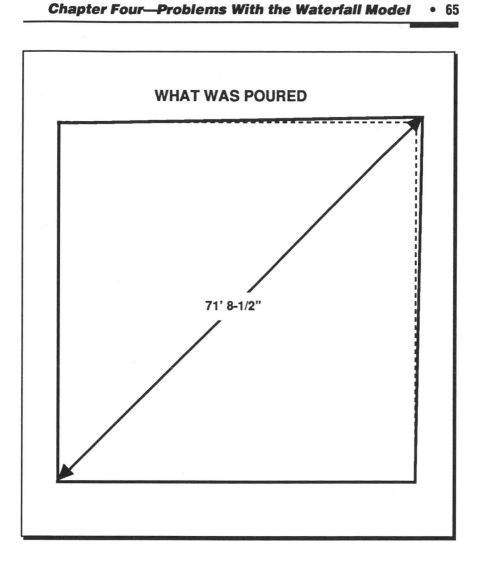

Figure 4-2b. The Actual Foundation

Now, suppose the company for which you are working wants you to write an application for personnel that advises employees about their benefits, including their retirement plan. The company offers a retirement plan and a "401K" tax-deferred savings plan as employee benefits. Part of your job is to advise the participants of how much money will be in the fund at their first opportunity to withdraw money without penalty. You are told that the first opportunity will be at the employee's sixtieth birthday. However, after the system is in test, you discover that the first opportunity is really when an employee reaches the age of fifty-nine and a half. The correction to the program will very likely be to change a few numbers in a conditional statement such as the following:

```
IF (EMPLOYEE_AGE .GTE. 60) THEN
    statement next
    statement next
    statement next
ENDIF
```

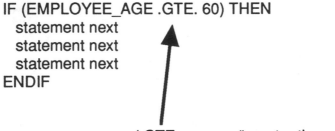

(.GTE. means: "greater than or equal to")

to

```
IF (EMPLOYEE_AGE .GTE. 59.5) THEN
    statement next
    statement next
    statement next
ENDIF
```

Obviously, there is not much work involved in correcting this mistake, at least from the casual observer's point of view.

However, from the developer's point of view, things could be more complicated. You might have been doing integer arithmetic. Now you have to do rational number arithmetic. Or, in order to continue using integer arithmetic, you now have to convert all the ages to months and worry about whether to round up or down. In addition, perhaps the sixtieth year was used for other purposes, such as the earliest age at which an employee can elect to retire. Now, you have to separate those numbers, *if* you can remember how they were combined in the first place.

Also, this does not take into account all of the intermediate products, such as the requirements or design documents, that have to be changed and the problems that could occur if all of the changes are not found.

These two errors are on about the same scale and, I would guess, cause about the same level of headache. However, the customer can *see* the former and not the latter. To the customer, the changes to the latter are more like making changes on blueprints rather than on actual concrete. As a result, users tend to change requirements on the fly. There is a report about a developer who was able to prevent downstream changes, but he probably had to keep the customers bound and gagged to do so.

I do not think these problems are show stoppers or even necessarily important. They are more matters of definition or dogma, like arguments for clerics in a monastery, rather than decisions for workers in the field.

But, there are serious internal problems with the Waterfall, and some of them *are* show stoppers. Some of these problems are listed below:

- Requirements (or specifications, depending upon your denominational preference) are incomplete.

- The Waterfall is very expensive to use.

- It takes a long, long time.

- It has many variations that really do not map into one another.

- It encourages a communications gap between the end users and the developers.

- It assumes that the "what" can be separated from the "how."

- It does not lend itself to proper error management and access to appropriate emerging technology.

- And, finally, it cannot be applied very well to a certain numerous class of problems.

We will now examine each of these problems in turn.

Incomplete Requirements

Having incomplete requirements makes developers crazy and is, perhaps, the most vexing problem besetting us. Analysis shows that incomplete requirements causes downstream costs to increase exponentially [Boehm 1981, p.40]. (See Figure 4-3.)

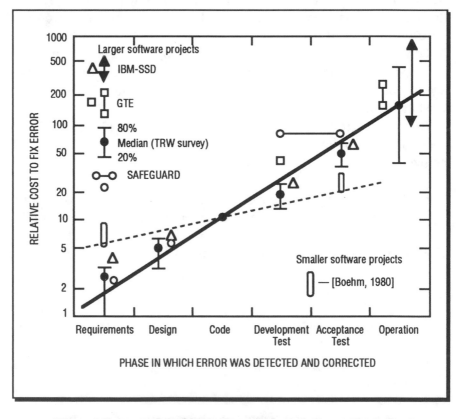

Figure 4-3. Increase in Cost to Fix or Change Software Throughout the Life Cycle

Many techniques have been developed to address this issue but, still, requirements are often incomplete.

I think we are asking the wrong question here. It is not, "*how do we get* complete requirements?" but, rather, "*can we get* complete requirements?" My answer is no. We are lucky to get 90% of the most important ones. There are many reasons for this.

First, just having computers in the environment affects the requirements. A small example is the effect of the "footprint" of PCs on the customers' work surfaces. Until the customers get their machines, how can they know the effect on their available work space?

A second reason is the "report effect." The customers are not entirely aware of what the computing systems will do for them, and they see new requirements as soon as old ones are met. They get one kind of report, and then ask whether you can now make it do this or that.

Third, as stated before, customers do not have the cautionary intermediate products to make them wary. And, they often need these intermediate results to make up their minds about what they *really* need in the first place.

In other words, intermediate results are needed not only to supply the necessary curbs on the customers' wishes, but also to provide information the customers really need in order to be clear about their requirements.

Fourth, people just are not used to completely specifying things. For example, when you buy a car, do you specify every nut and bolt in it? Even very large purchases, for example, modern commercial jet aircraft, which are routinely specified in great detail by very knowledgeable people, do not have *all* the detail or the *level* of detail we expect from computer-system customers. Many, many details are covered by standards, and many specifications are bound up into mega specs.

Why do changing requirements vex us so much in our business? I think part of the answer is that software is invisible to us. It is like traveling across the Antarctic ice sheet where Nature provides few landmarks to guide us on our way. We travelers must provide our own landmarks and, if we are not careful, we can lose our way.

The landmarks we provide for software development require that we proceed straight through, without having to go back. But, if we must turn back or if we are diverted, then we can lose our way. Although we may eventually make it to the far side, we leave behind us many mistakes, cost overruns, incomplete work, and other evidence of floundering. One of the things that will cause us to go back is a change in requirements; hence, our need for unchanging requirements. This need for certainty is brought about by a profound uncertainty about our work because we have not yet been able to clearly mark the way.

It Costs Too Much

The Waterfall model was introduced in our field during an era when there were fewer computers than computer programmers, and when a person's time was relatively less expensive than the computer's time. It was necessary to plan and work very carefully in order to optimize the time and space required to run our programs and, more importantly, to minimize the time to get our programs running on the computer.

In that environment, the overall cost was minimized by doing extensive work at the desk: planning, analyzing, designing, coding, and code checking. SADP replaced the informal desk procedures with formal ones.

Now, however, computer time is extremely cheap compared to a programmer's time, and rather than let the computers locate our mistakes and otherwise pick up after us, we are still expected to use methods applicable to another era.

Understandably, learning the formal methods (the Waterfall and SADP) was costly. But, using them in actual projects was more costly than the informal methods they replaced. Front end activities became longer. Requirements involved creating current and new logical and physical models and documenting them. Even if analysts did not use structured analysis and design, they still had to collect and maintain much more data than they were used to in the code-and-go shops, especially on larger projects.

One of the most popular forms of data collection was the customer interview. These interviews were used during the code-and-go era and formalized during the SADP era. With less formal code-and-go methods, the gist of the conversation was remembered by the analyst and no recording or approval was needed. But, many observers thought that too many requirements slipped through the cracks. So, formal interviews, along with other more formal methods, were introduced. Conducting the interviews was costly, because of the time involved in conducting the interviews and the number of people tied up in conducting them. Added to the cost was typing the notes, getting them reviewed and approved by the interviewee, and then keeping and maintaining the notes. And, there was still no guarantee that there were no misunderstandings or that the information was useful. It was my impression (and many correspondents agreed) that these interviews were more proforma than useful.

In addition to the costs of data collection, there are data flow diagrams, structure charts, data dictionaries, and other documentation that have to be created and maintained. There were no tools at first to help us. So, although structured methods were expected to be used, few programmers actually had time to do the work that was now required of them.

Yet, in spite of these new methods, requirements continued to change. Attempting to keep up with them or keep them constant led to yet more documentation to save and maintain. So, as you proceeded down through the Waterfall, you accreted an ever-increasing mass of material that required more and more resources to maintain.

Albert Case talks about this in his article in the August, 1987, issue of System Development. "The assertion of reduced project completion time (that is, improved developer efficiency) is justified by the fact that structured techniques result in a validated system specification which reduces coding and testing time. [**Author's note:** Here, I use structured methods and the Waterfall together. Albert Case does not explicitly do this, but it is reasonable to assume that SADP is consistent with the Waterfall, as I argue above.] In some instances this is true. However, in some organizations specifications consist of notes written on the back of napkins and design is done at the terminal using COBOL, FORTRAN, or some other specification technique. In these "code-and-go" shops, the documentation requirements of a structured technique can easily equal the time required to code and test the system. [**Author's note:** There is a study that computes all the work up through design at 51.3% of the total. See: *A Survey of Software Engineering Practice: Tools, Methods, and Results*, Beck, L.L., and Perkins, T.E., IEEE Transactions on Software Engineering, Vol. SE-9, No. 5, September, 1983, p.545.] Even if 50% of the coding and testing can be eliminated as a result of a high quality specification, the net project time has still been extended. For example, using traditional code-and-go methods, a project may take 1,000 hours to complete. Analysis and design using structured methods can easily take 1,000 hours, while reduced programming and testing now amount to 500 hours. The project using structured techniques now requires 1,500 hours or a net 50% increase. Clearly, by altering the parameters, structured techniques [would] fare better. If any other non-structured methodology were used, and replaced with structured analysis and design, net decreases are possible."

One way of managing this is to freeze the requirements, produce an initial system, collect changes and release another version, and then repeat the cycle. It works, and is a very popular way of doing business. However, the documentation usually suffers as a result of this process. My correspondents report that upstream documentation seldom matches the semi-final product. And yet, a complete and unambiguous specification for the system is touted as the main reason for using the Waterfall.

Often, the organizations using the software are aware of this problem and set about getting their requirements "right." Since they often have no constraints of time or money from the upstream processes, and they do not get cautionary intermediate products until way down stream, they produce a gargantuan requirements document listing everything they can think of, including the kitchen sink. Often called a "Victorian novel," this document overwhelms the developers and becomes the basis for inter-organizational squabbling later on when the project falls out of bed and it is time for finger pointing.

One of my correspondents said that if the decision makers involved had set the cost and schedule limitations when they first initiated the project, paring down the Victorian novels wouldn't be as difficult later on.

Proponents of the Waterfall assume that these costs will be recovered in lower maintenance costs downstream. But, wouldn't it be better if the method you are applying now is effective in its own right, and does not depend on some future events for its success?

Besides, there seems to be a neat little conspiracy here. Maintenance is always somebody else's problem; it is usually done by junior developers who want to get out of maintenance and on up their career paths. So, these proponents and decision makers simply assert that there will be lower maintenance costs, and go on to the next project. If anybody pays attention to the costs later on, then the high costs can be blamed on the junior people.

In addition, the assumption about lower downstream costs is problematic. Consider, for example, the reliability of the system. Reliability is an indicator of maintenance activity: the more reliable the system, the less maintenance there is. One study by Card and others [1987] tried to assess the effect of software engineering technologies on reliability. They found that top-down development (the Waterfall) and structured code had practically no effect on reliability. The major factors affecting reliability were quality assurance, documentation, and code readings (reviews).

The investigators admitted that it is difficult to assess the effect of a technology on software development. In their investigation, they needed to account for non-technology factors and ended up with a small sample of programs written in one language. The value of the results might be argued about, justifiably.

Here are some more data points: Boehm found that the escalating cost to fix of smaller, less formal projects was about 100 times less than for large, more formal ones. [Boehm 1981, p.40. See also Figure 4-3.]

There is another study to look at. [Vessey and Weber 1984, p.403] The samples in this study are much larger than the Card et al. study. From laboratory studies: "In summary, the results of the laboratory studies on structured programming are equivocal." [ibid] In field studies: "For the U.S. organizations neither top-down design nor the control structures had any effect [on productivity]." [ibid, p.404] In another study of 278 programs: "He found no evidence in support of top-down design or structured control constructs as a means of increasing programmer productivity." [ibid, p.404] In another study of 353 COBOL programs: "She found no evidence to support the use of structured programming." [ibid, p.404]

The point I want to make here is not that top-down development and structured code are unequivocally *bad*, but that claims for them being unequivocally *good* are not always supported by the data our scientists collect. Formal methods must stand in their own right as effective ways of developing software, and not as harbingers of good times ahead.

In summary, formal methods often increase the costs of producing software over the methods they replace. It remains to be seen whether or not they have beneficial effects later on.

It Takes Too Long

With the Waterfall model, there is no useful output until way into the project, the commitment, and the funding. This makes people nervous. Management complains: "When are we going to get some return on our investment?" Government agencies, who know all about long lead times, tend to encourage long development schedules by demanding many intermediate "deliverables," each of which must be produced according to some format and go through some signing ceremony. We end up talking about the project rather than doing the project.

This is not only the fault of the model; there is some mystery and invisibility in our work that makes managers and buyers, especially cost-conscious government buyers, uneasy. But this model, with its stately progression through the phases, does not lend itself to rapid development. All of the paperwork and all of the signatures mitigate against it.

One Waterfall model I analyzed was composed of 114 major tasks, across 87 different organizations, with 39 deliverables, and 164 authorizations, for a total of over 400 important items on which to spend time.

Most of these deliverable documents act as "wampum" throughout the life of the project in that people *think* they have intrinsic value when, in fact, they do not. As wampum, these documents allow people to *talk* about the project, but not actually *do* the project. In reality, the deliverable documents only have value if the system is completed, just as wampum only has value if someone is willing to accept it in trade. However, the *plan* for the project is treated as if it has as much value as *doing* the project, with people often staking their reputations and careers on the *plan.* The authorizations become mere ceremonies in which the guilt is transferred from one organization to another.

One of my correspondents listed four major projects on which he had worked. Every one of them were years in length, and at least one year longer than estimated when the design reviews were conducted, which were themselves already a long way into the project.

The effect of the timeliness of production is seen when the project encounters the business-decision "horizon." For most businesses, there is an expectation that any activity that is engaged in to increase capacity or productivity should take from two to three years. A new plant, for example, can usually be constructed in about this period of time. This is the business-decision horizon: the length of time to which the business feels it can commit itself for the planned activity. However, much planning and money are spent on the purchase of the site, obtaining permits, developing architectural plans, etc., *before* the actual construction begins. These activities are not included in the actual construction.

In our business, analogous preliminary activities are included as part of the actual project. As a result, the Waterfall includes a lot more than it should. But, management often does not see that the model covers too much, treating the process as they would when constructing a new plant.

For example, when starting the construction of a new plant, the site has already been selected, paid for, and an environmental impact study has at least been initiated before the construction project commences. But, in the Waterfall model, the equivalent steps are *part* of the project. What management sees as construction of a new plant is essentially the same as the *construction* of a new system, which is step 5 (Coding) of the Waterfall model.

You can see that management often does not realize what it is letting itself in for. Since so many requirements and details are included in the Waterfall model (causing the project to take much too long), management goes crazy.

Suppose, however, that some activity equivalent to searching for a new plant, etc., occurred *outside* the Waterfall model. Management would then see the rest of the activities as being basically the same as all the activities required in obtaining a new plant. These initial activities are what is done in "system engineering." A truncated Waterfall model is just one of the elements of this process.

Extended development times can adversely affect the quality of the system; paradoxically, I would suggest, since one of the reasons for spending all that time is to ensure high quality. Some time ago, I was in the office of a computing-system user. She had several terminals next to her desk, and would be considered an experienced user. She seemed somewhat distracted and, when I asked, she told me that she had just attended a training session for a new system and it upset her. She concluded that the new system was designed for programmers, not for "regular" people.

I knew something about this system. One of my correspondents, who had worked on it, described it as having incomplete requirements. He said it was a "moving target." In addition, it had a fixed completion date with no limitation on the size of the system and was largely staffed by inexperienced analysts and programmers. I knew several people on the project. True, there were some inexperienced folks doing the work, but they were good workers: P_as of the type that would eventually become professionals.

The real problem with this system was its business horizon: early set and inflexible. As time grew short, the designers ended up producing as if the users were as knowledgeable as they were. [Ledgard 1987] And, the result was the remark and personal experience of the user described above. If it takes too long, the Waterfall will be foreshortened and the users will end up paying for it.

In my opinion, if there were to be a fixed completion date, which I recommend as a good start, there must be associated with it some sizing and scheduling rules necessary to ensure adequate resources for each step. That is what one of my correspondents referred to earlier. The designers in my example did not have the time resources necessary to produce a good user interface.

Finally, the fact that this model's costs are high is a good indicator that it takes too long. The staff burns up budget whether it is producing software or reports.

Variations

Many variations of the Waterfall do not map into one another, even though proponents of it still think they do. [McCracken and Jackson 1982] A six-phase cycle really is different from a nine-phase cycle. Usually the difference is reflected in the context within which the model is operating.

The NASA six-phase cycle operates within a system development cycle, while the nine-phase business model operates in a standalone mode. The starting and ending points are different. The six-phase model is already way downstream in the system development cycle, and many opportunities have arisen to constrain it in money, length, performance, etc. No such opportunities naturally arise in the nine-phase model: these have to be determined (if they ever are) internally, mainly by the experience and wisdom of the initiators.

The activities among the phases are described differently. And, because the contexts are different, there is more divergence from a common understanding of terms. A manager from a DoD project really talks a different language than one from an MIS shop.

The result is a rather broad front of support for the Waterfall in the face of obvious problems in producing software in a timely and efficient manner. At least the engineering folks are talking to the business folks about common aspects of their work. But, this support does not allow for many critical looks at the model. It is somewhat like the misbehaving child whose parents do not believe he misbehaves because they have not paid much attention to how he acts around other people. They only believe he is good because that is the way he behaves around them.

End-User Communications Gap

The variations problem is nothing compared to problem of communications inside the Waterfall itself. As McCracken has said: "The life cycle concept [referring to the Waterfall] perpetuates our failure so far, as an industry, to build an effective bridge across the communication gap between end user and systems analysts ... What we understand to be the conventional life cycle approach might be compared with a supermarket at which the customer is forced to provide a complete order to a stock clerk at the door of the store with no opportunity to roam the aisles—comparing prices, remembering items not on the shopping list or getting a headache and deciding to go out for dinner ... ." [McCracken and Jackson 1982]

The converse is also true. A common complaint I receive is lack of participation by the customer in important decisions until it is too late. Many end users, especially the unsophisticated ones, expect not to have to roam the aisles of the supermarket. They also expect that the developers know a lot more about the problem than they are told by the end user. So, after significant development is done, the user rejects some or all of the software, which causes overruns, long periods of overtime by the development staff, and an inclination by management to exert more pressure on the development staff increasing the stress.

There are also communications gaps within the development team, mainly due to the horizontal integration of the work. In a horizontally integrated project, one specialist performs his tasks on one project, and then goes on to another project on which he performs the same tasks. For example, if a programmer is working on 10 concurrent projects, the tasks he performs on Project 1 he also performs on Project 2, and then on Project 3, and so on, working his way horizontally all the way across the projects.

There are many opportunities for miscommunication with this procedure, and similar errors can be introduced across all the projects. Since horizontally integrated projects tend not to have much review, especially from upstream and downstream team members, there are fewer chances for errors to be caught during the reviews. Therefore, the process is not self correcting.

In a vertically integrated project, however, the opposite is true. Tasks flow into one another, enabling the programmer to look forward and backward to succeeding and preceding phases. Therefore, there tends to be more review, and this makes the process more self correcting.

Here are some of the layers that I know about, each with its own set of specialists: The initiators (those who propose that the project be undertaken), the problem definers (the end users), the systems analysts, designers, coders, testers and, finally, the maintenance people. (See Figure 4-4). Each of these layers corresponds roughly to a phase of the Waterfall, each has its own boundary and, therefore, a rich opportunity for misunderstandings. The effect of the communications gap is, first, an incomplete set of requirements and then, as the project proceeds, incomplete transfer from one phase to another.

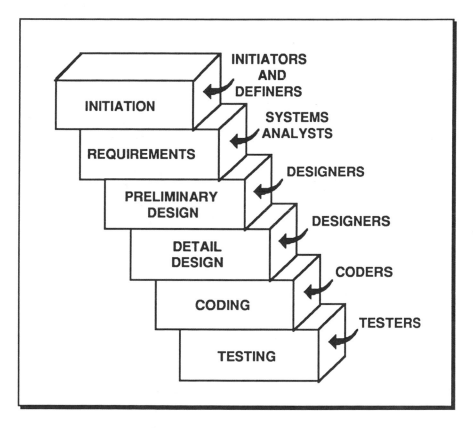

Figure 4-4. The Layers of Tasks

One of my correspondents, who described his successful project, attributes its success to excellent communications among the team members who were integrated vertically. The problems began to occur in the Maintenance phase because the maintenance people were not on the team: They inherited the software from the development team. He said that because everything else had gone so well, the problems with the maintenance people came as a big surprise.

The "What" Separated from the "How"

There is an assumption in the Waterfall model, and in the structured analysis and design associated with it, that the problem description can be isolated from the problem solution. [Zave 1986] This has shown up in the horizontal integration mentioned earlier. The idea of postponing solutions until the problem is defined is also one of the tenets of structured analysis and design. Again, this is a logical assumption. Unfortunately, real people do not behave that way. Ordinarily, people consider a range of possible solutions when they consider problems.

There are some advantages to bringing up a range of solutions early, especially if they are well known. For example, it helps to clarify the problem, revealing aspects that might not otherwise be thought of until much later. Also, it helps to constrain costs to know in what general direction you are going. And, it helps with expectations, gives a feeling of confidence, and reduces the number of nasty surprises.

Trying to enforce a non-implementation attitude leads to misunderstandings in the handoff between the analyst and the designer. (See Figure 4-5.)

Error Management

There is an error-management difficulty inherent in all top-down models, including the Waterfall. [McFarland 1986] One cannot predict in advance how to handle all error modes and must, therefore, have an incomplete detailed design. Difficulties here reflect all the way back up the chain. Not only error management, but certain characteristics of the hardware such as response times, overhead for backup and accounting, traffic control, etc., cannot be known in advance if consideration of the solution is deferred until the last—and these have implications for requirements.

McFarland puts it this way: "During the definition of a module's function and interface it is possible to define certain error situations that may arise. However, defining the internal response to these errors would imply that the designer is considering the implementation details of the modules. This is a violation of the abstraction principle and is inappropriate. In addition, designers cannot be

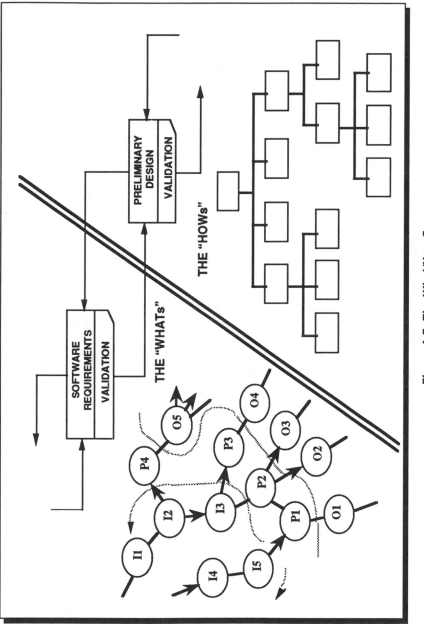

Figure 4-5. The What/How Gap

cognizant of all the possible errors a module may generate. Accordingly, at the outset, the response to these errors will also be unknown. Therefore, there is a considerable potential that the interface of a module will be changed after that interface has been defined and used during earlier design activities."

Wicked Problems

The Waterfall model has been associated with software projects that put the computer at the center of things: the payroll system, the airline reservation system, the planning system, etc. In these systems, humans serve the machine, providing it with the inputs it needs to produce the results. But, we are now encountering problems of a different nature where the computer is no longer at the center of things—the human is—and the machine is now acting to provide or organize information the humans need to produce results. These are called "wicked" problems, described by Horst Rittel and Melvin Webber [1973].

There are many aspects to wicked problems. Some bear directly on problems of using the Waterfall model—others show tantalizing sides of these problems for computer professionals to help solve.

The opposite of wicked problems are "righteous" problems. These can be defined, data about them can be collected and analyzed, and a solution can be constructed. This is the procedure of the Waterfall. (See Figure 4-6.)

On the other hand, "wicked problems do not have a definite formulation." [Rittel and Webber 1973] Another way of saying this is that some of the solution space lies within the problem space. (See Figure 4-7.) The problem is fully understood only *after* it is solved. This means that intermediate results must be obtained *before* a final solution can be reached, or that the problem is defined and solved at the same time.

There are many examples of this aspect of wicked problems. Every time you have a user who is not sure about what he wants and needs a preliminary idea of what the solution will look like, you have a wicked problem. There is no use beating on him: he simply needs intermediate results like so many of us do when we are engaged in trying to obtain something new with little to go on.

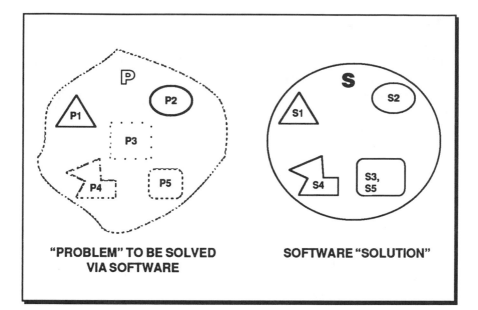

Figure 4-6. Righteous Problems

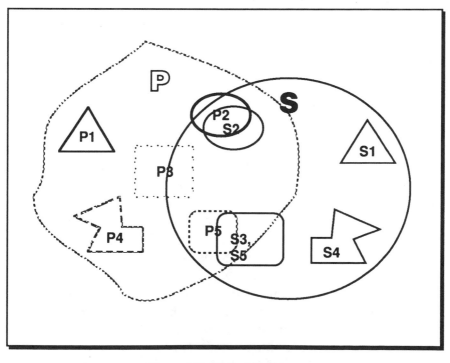

Figure 4-7. Wicked Problems

In engineering, there are algorithms that produce a solution by successive approximation, similar to the situation above. They are composed of a calculating part and a comparing part. You start off with an initial guess about the solution and some criteria about what a solution would look like. The calculating part goes into action and produces a result and an indication of how far off the mark you are. This is called the error. Then, the comparing part goes to work and compares the error with the solution criteria. If the error does not meet the criteria, then the result that was just calculated becomes the new guess for another iteration through the algorithm. This proceeds until the error falls within the criteria. Then, the results become the solution. Notice that each iteration starts with the intermediate results from the previous one.

Sometimes, the procedure does not work and the error increases with each iteration. Then, you must change your initial guess, change the solution criteria, or find another algorithm.

There is a similar procedure in the consumer software market. We produce a word processor, take it to market, and wait for feedback, which provides the initial results. This feedback is in the form of revenue, product reviews, complaints, and suggestions. It tells us whether or not we have at least partially solved the problem of producing an acceptable word processor. If the revenue is too low, we consider leaving the market, redesigning the product, or addressing a different niche. If the revenue is acceptable, we use the other feedback to develop the next version, and so on. When we finally leave the word processor market, our solution will be the last version, not the first. My correspondents in the consumer market tell me that although they start off with a "specification," they do not maintain it. It is a "seed" document, and the current specifications are in the source code of the product.

Another example is a medical diagnosis application. The application usually starts off with an initial set of symptoms and test results. For example, the patient's symptoms could be tearing eyes and a headache. This symptom is then entered together with the patient's temperature, blood pressure, and heart rate. The application then tries to find the diagnosis that matches, but will probably produce several since the symptoms are rather vague. It then asks for more information so that it can narrow down the list, and then repeats the process until there is only one diagnosis remaining. This becomes the suggested diagnosis for the patient.

However, I do not think there will be coin-operated "doctor machines" in every drugstore soon, even if they were 100% correct all the time. The diagnosis is only *part* of the solution to the patient's problem. Collecting the information, asking the right questions, and performing the appropriate tests still must be done by the doctor. But, notice here how the machine becomes an *aid to* the doctor rather than a *replacement for* the doctor.

Wicked problems are often not easy to spot. In our training classes, we are often presented with sample problems that have marvelous solutions. These can include very wicked problems, but their solutions have already been discovered through many painful processes. By the time we get into class, the problems have already been solved and neatly tied up. This makes it difficult to determine that the problems were wicked ones in the first place. But, these solutions are always seen in retrospect, *after* the solution is known to exist and has already been refined. But what about problems considered the other way around—when it isn't known yet whether this even *is* a solution, much less what the solution is. Without the pre-packaged solutions, the problem might indeed turn out to be a wicked one. If we consider the kinds of problems that we get in school as solvable, when we get into the real world we find that the first crack at a solution can be much more difficult than it first appeared.

The Waterfall has a hard time with wicked problems because it is difficult to make the Waterfall iterate. It must be based on a complete set of unambiguous requirements.

"Wicked problems have no stopping rules." [ibid] Work stops for external reasons such as lack of time, money, or patience. Also, the problems are not solved, but only have degrees of sufficiency.

SDI is an example of a wicked problem because of the extremely high cost and large technological and, some say, geo-political risks. Already it has been scaled back from the original concept. Other examples of wicked problems are programs involving new algorithms, which require constant checking and tinkering, systems involving uncertain business conditions, systems involving incomplete information about the environment, very large problems, and very complex problems. These last two are "wicked" if there are no size or complexity-management functions in place to control them.

Now, it might be argued that the Waterfall would bring size and complexity control to the development, but this is not so. It would bring systemization and orderliness, but these are not sufficient to manage size or complexity.

For example, consider the requirements document for a very large system. According to the theory, *all* the requirements would be in the document. The document is then passed to the developers to implement. But, they must read the document to know what the requirements are. The larger the system the larger the document until, finally, a system is so large that its requirements document defies human comprehension. This would result in developers using all of their time trying to understand the requirements. Nothing would get done and some outside agent would have to stop the thing.

Something like this also occurs in government circles when relatively simple and straightforward systems are overburdened with requirements by departmental politics. This inevitably causes the project to fail or results in requirements being skipped or partially implemented.

There was a time when an important part of a programmer's job was to minimize the number of machine cycles and the amount of memory required to run the program. For many of us, machine cycles and memory are relatively cheap and plentiful and we do not worry about those factors. But, with embedded systems and other small computers, this is still a problem. However, notice some of the stopping rules: "That's fast enough" or "That's small enough." They are arbitrary and external to the problem itself.

"Solutions to wicked problems are not true-or-false but good-or-bad." [ibid] In other words, there are no objective, unambiguous criteria for deciding if the problem is solved. In our business, we have many similar problems.

"Make or buy" decisions are frequently like that. Not only is there the problem of whether or not you have enough information, but also whether the information you have is appropriate. Do we really have the skills to do the job or is that what we advertise? Can we really buy it for less or is that smoke and mirrors from the vendor? Do we make our decisions just to get along with other members of our team or do we make them based on the technical merits?

How many times have you heard: "Nobody ever lost their job for buying Big Blue." Now, IBM produces very fine products and is well known for its service. But, it is not the *only* producer of good computer products. If, however, your corporate culture has bought into one vendor or another, then it would be "prudent" for you to seriously consider that vendor when you are making the buying decisions.

Take, for example, the controversy between the Macintosh and IBM PC. Proponents for both sides argue about the "goodness" of their candidate and the "badness" of the other. We have no objective criteria for determining which is correct (at least not until Chapter Nine, where I will offer some). The arguments take on moral overtones, and one machine is selected over another in order to be on the side of the angels, rather than find a solution to the age-old human problem of using technology. "Mac-bigots" and "PC-bigots" are terms frequently heard and used to mean personal, subjective preferences rather than objective ones. Now, I am all for allowing personal preferences to have some weight, but I do not want to be required to use someone elses'.

Wrapped up in the "goodness/badness" controversy is the fact that, for some reason, there is a lack of reality checking. Here is an example: In 1985, I once was listening to a discussion between two big shots about *standard* hardware for their organization. At this time, the IBM PC and its clones were *standard* and were on the *preferred* equipment list. This meant that it was easier and quicker to purchase them than other equipment. These big shots were discussing the reasons why Macintoshes were not on the list, and had to be ordered and justified on a case-by-case basis. Their main objection, at least during the discussion I was listening to, was that Macs could not communicate with other machines and the strategic plan required that workstations be able to do this (apparently a reasonable objection).

I was standing between the two and could see into an office about thirty feet away. There, on the desk, was a Macintosh that was obviously connected to a mainframe because it was displaying the electronic mail screen. When I pointed out that *there* was one Mac hooked up to a mainframe, he said that it had to be directly connected "like with an IRMA board," not through a modem. So, his argument really was not that the Mac *could not* communicate, but that it was not like a PC.

In software development, wherever there are political or turf issues in problems to be solved, solutions take on this moral flavor. We are building this software for moral reasons, not for technical ones.

Suppose your organization decides to build a "universal" workstation to be used by any programmer in any environment. Of course, there is the problem of deciding what one of those "universal" workstations is. So, you get all the different types of programmers and folks from each kind of environment together to figure this thing out.

Suppose that the guy from business systems has the most influence and the workstation is designed according to his notions. Also suppose that management buys into this design. Now, when the objections about the applicability of the design to other environments are overruled for "business" reasons, you are dealing with a moral issue, which is a wicked problem.

"There is no immediate and no ultimate test of a solution to a wicked problem. For tame problems ... the test of a solution is entirely under the control of the few people who are involved and interested in the problem.

"With wicked problems, on the other hand, any solution, after being implemented, will generate waves of consequences over an extended—virtually—unbounded period of time. Moreover, the next day's consequences of the solution may yield utterly undesirable repercussions which outweigh the intended advantages or the advantages accomplished hitherto. In such cases, one would have been better off if the plan had never been carried out." [ibid]

An example of this is a computer virus, where pieces of code perform a simple function and replicate themselves in the systems they encounter. They may have been created for innocent and friendly reasons such as saying hello, wishing users happy holiday, or giving them useful information, like the location of a good bulletin board. But, the consequences have been horrendous for some and uncomfortable for most of us. They may not have known it, but the creators of viruses have encountered *wicked* wicked problems. And, this kind of software has taken on ethical, if not true moral, tones.

Another example appears to be the cumulative effect of stock market software which, some say, exacerbates fluctuations in buying and selling trends and helped bring on the crash of 87. There, a solution for some investors' problems with investing strategies became the cause of greater problems for the investors and everybody else when too many people used and followed the dictates of the software.

It also has had the effect of requiring investors to use computers to manage their investing activities in order to "keep up." At $5,000 per "investor workstation," you now have a barrier to entry into the investment market that did not exist before.

"Every solution to a wicked problem is a 'one-shot operation'; because there is no opportunity to learn by trial-and-error, every attempt counts significantly.

"In the sciences and fields like mathematics, chess, puzzle-solving or mechanical engineering design, the problem solver can try various runs without penalty. Whatever his outcome on these individual runs, it doesn't matter much to the subject-system or to the course of societal affairs. A lost chess game is seldom consequential for other chess games or for chess players.

"With wicked ... problems, however, every implemented solution is consequential. It leaves 'traces' that cannot be undone. One cannot build a freeway to see how it works, and then easily correct it after unsatisfactory performance. Large public works are effectively irreversible, and the consequences they generate have long half-lives. Many people's lives will have been irreversibly influenced, and large amounts of money will have been spent—another irreversible act. The same happens with most other large-scale public works and with virtually all public-service programs. The effects of an experimental curriculum will follow the pupils into their adult lives.

"Whenever actions are effectively irreversible and whenever the half-lives of the consequences are long, every trial counts. And every attempt to reverse a decision or to correct for the undesired consequences poses another set of wicked problems which are in turn subject to the same dilemma." [ibid]

An example of how computing can help solve this kind of problem is with highway planning software. Such software enables planners to, in effect, build a freeway to see how it works, and then easily correct it after unsatisfactory performance.

Now, you could try to use a Waterfall here. It would be easy enough to specify many elements of the problem up front, such as population centers, rivers, mountains, etc. There are even algorithms that are useful for modelling traffic flow, such as the fluid flow equations from physics.

But, to make the model work, you have to tune it in the environment where the highway will be built. Here is some information that will be needed: How viscously (easily) will the traffic flow on this highway for commuters? How will morning and evening sun positions affect vision, speed, and the number of accidents? What will the smog patterns be? How will population patterns change?

All of this information has effects on traffic patterns and must be fed back into the program to modify the results. This tuning occurs *after* the application is in use and requires intermediate and perhaps new functions for each case. You cannot know all this stuff in advance. But, you *can* build flexible programs that allow you to add new information and functions as they occur in actual use.

"Wicked problems do not have an enumerable (or an exhaustively describable) set of potential solutions, nor is there a well-described set of permissible operations that may be incorporated into the [solution]." [ibid] Here, expert systems can help extract a *best* set of solutions and operations.

I recently used a "knowledge-based system" to create an "application" to help me understand a procedure for performing the "make or buy" decision. I started by putting in a few of the simple considerations and described them in simple ways. I ran the application and got a result. Then, I added more and more considerations and described them in more and more complex ways. Still, I got results; perhaps a little different, but nonetheless results. I would say, however, that the *quality* of the results improved as I made my application more and more like the procedure and the real world circumstances the procedure is expected to be used in. I could continue this process indefinitely, getting solutions slightly different each time.

But, another important aspect of this was that the programmers, who maintained the knowledge-based system, used the feedback I gave them to improve the program that produced my application! To a large extent, they based their development on getting intermediate results from users on a working system.

"Every wicked problem is essentially unique." [ibid] Although two problems may seem similar on the surface, their differences might overwhelm the similarities. In the highway example above, perhaps the most important consideration is a bridge that must be built across a waterway that has not been bridged before.

The planning software might not be up to the siting task unless it has new functionality added. And, after it is added, the software would then encounter, from information about the potential sites, new and unique characteristics about the sites that could swamp inflexible programs.

For example, suppose that while your software is dutifully predicting traffic flows on the waterway below, a question is raised by some of the highway planners about the suspension towers on the bridge. They are concerned that these towers might be hazardous to aviation going to and from the nearby airport. As you can see, other factors can add to the scope of a problem, requiring more functionality to solve a new problem, that you could not have considered before.

"Every wicked problem can be considered a symptom of another problem. ... If we recognize deficient mental health services as part of the problem of crime in the streets, then—trivially enough—improvement of mental health services is a specification of solution. If, as the next step, we declare the lack of community centers one deficiency of the mental health services system, then procurement of community centers is the next specification of solution. If it is inadequate treatment within community centers, then improved therapy training of staff may be the locus of solution, and so on." [ibid]

"The existence of a discrepancy representing a wicked problem can be explained in numerous ways. The choice of explanation determines the nature of the problem's resolution." [ibid] Problems in the social or political arena tend to have a characteristic where the policy that is put into effect comes from the problem description of the person who won the election. Here, a computer can help by assisting people in clarifying their information and ideas. However, the computer cannot provide "the" answer. Fortunately, that is still for people to do.

"The [problem solver] has no right to be wrong." [ibid] In science, hypotheses are valued only as they stand up to refutation. Science can be seen as grinding out refutations to theories, improving the confidence we can have in information we hold to be true.

But, in the social world, we often cannot wait that long. Science might require that we continue to do "double blind" testing of potential cures for disease. But, in the face of numerous deaths and increasing death-rates, other solutions must be tried. It will be urged t_ try drugs that seem to hold promise from laboratory tests, but which have not been clinically tested. So, they will be tried in an environment where the information is hazy.

With a particular patient, the doctor has probably one or two shots at helping him and the consequences of his work cannot be predicted. Here, computers can aid in the process by creating simulators on which to try drugs, to help medical researchers make trial runs, and to gain experience with potential cures. But, the ability to simulate biological systems in a computer requires intermediate results in order to gain needed information to improve the model.

However, if we had good biological simulators, then drugs could be quickly checked to see what value they might have. While the usual scientific process must still be observed, in those cases where timeliness is most important and these untested drugs are tried as a last resort, doctors would have better information to go on.

Finally, there is an aspect to wicked problems that Rittel and Webber have not commented on but which, I hope, they would agree on. It is that many projects, which ought not be attempted, nevertheless are attempted and with bad results. These are the "boondoggles." Many of them proceed because of the "Abilene Paradox" discovered and named by Jerry Harvey [1988]. He noticed that sometimes "... organization members make collective decisions that lead them to take actions *contrary* to what they want to do, and thereby arrive at results that are counterproductive to the organization's intent and purposes." [ibid, p.20] He gives several symptoms, but they add up to the notion that "You go along to get along."

Harvey offers suggestions for avoiding the paradox or escaping it once you are in it. For example, the age old sport of "shooting the messenger" should be discouraged.

Now, with software boondoggles using the Waterfall, it is often a long time before the paradox is noticed because it is often a long time before anything useable is produced. If we have a method for getting results sooner, then we stand a chance of noticing the paradox and doing something about it sooner.

Nevertheless, shooting the messenger should still be discouraged.

Final Thoughts and Summary

Some of my correspondents have objected that these problems are not daunting. They feel that I am unjustly "attacking" the Waterfall, pointing out that many projects have successfully used the Waterfall and that while there were some failures, we should blame some other aspect of the methodology, such as the management practices, rather than blaming the model itself. They offered both a long list of successes and, conversely, examples of failures with other models.

It is undoubtedly true that using the Waterfall helped many projects and was an improvement over the code-and-go shops of some years back. (**Author's note:** Here, I am using the term without the SADP connotation, because SADP is useful in its own right no matter how you actually develop the software.)

Yet many of the "success" stories they offered were viewed differently by other correspondents on the same projects, some of whom stated that "success" had been redefined so many times that the term became irrelevant.

Much of the time, success with the Waterfall model is not really success at all. Either the model used wasn't really the Waterfall model, or the notions that the defenders of this model have of success aren't what we developers would accept as success. And, when I questioned these correspondents about what model they actually used on their successful projects, they admitted that a "bastardized" version was employed to make the project work.

I am *not* saying that the Waterfall model cannot be used and is *never* any good. What I *am* saying is that the traditional view of it is seriously flawed. Many people understand its flaws and have tailored it to suit their purposes. Wouldn't it be nice, though, to work with a model that doesn't have these flaws to start with? Figure 4-8 is an illustration of the actual model they used. It is an interesting model, but I would not call it a Waterfall.

My correspondents are correct about one thing. I do intend to attack something, but it is not the Waterfall model. It is the dogmatic approach that so many people have taken concerning its applicability and effectiveness.

Dogmatism is not new to engineering and science, which is what we would like to be part of. One would have thought that we had escaped dogmatism when Galileo challenged the Ptolemaic view of the earth-centered world with his investigation of the heavens using a telescope. But, even in astronomy it continues to dog us. I will tell a little story about it to explain what I'm trying to accomplish here.

As the new view of the heavens became accepted, William Herschel discovered the seventh planet, Uranus, in 1781. In 1800, Freidrich Hegel, the noted philosopher, proved "that although the definition of planets had changed since the Ancients [sic], there could only be, philosophically, seven planets." [Bronowski 1973] On January 1, 1801, Giuseppe Piazzi discovered an eighth one, the minor planet, Ceres. "Hegel then seems to have returned to pursuits less amenable to disproof." [Sagan 1974]

Uranus' orbit didn't behave as expected, so yet another planet's existence was suspected. That led to the discovery of Neptune by Leverrier and Adams, working independently in 1846. But its orbit was troubling, and that is where Percival Lowell enters the story. Fascinated by an Italian astronomer's report of "canali" on Mars, Lowell had built an observatory near Flagstaff, Arizona, to observe them. He and his staff also made studies of other planets, including Neptune. He concluded that the eccentricity of Neptune's orbit was due to an unseen ninth planet, and organized a search for this missing planet that lasted past his death. Fourteen years later, a Lowell observatory staff member, Clyde Tombaugh, who got his job because of the excellence of his sketches of the canals on Mars, discovered the ninth planet, Pluto.

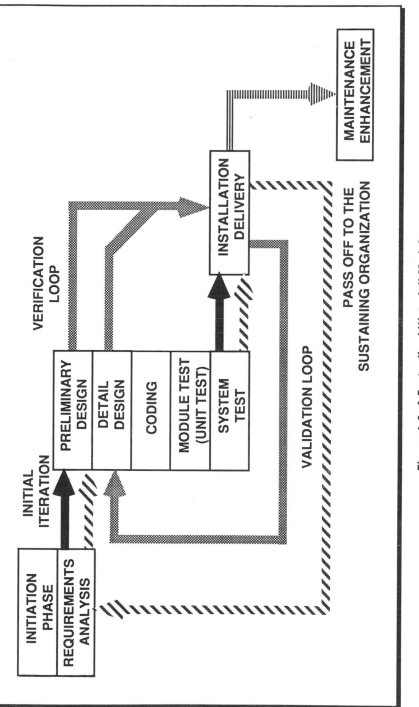

Figure 4-8. A Bastardized Waterfall Model

The dogmatism of Hegel led to nothing and helped no one. The errors of Lowell and Tombaugh (the belief of the existence of canals on Mars and what that implied) were part of a serious search for truth. This search resulted among other things in the discovery of Pluto.

Now, I am not attacking the Waterfall as such. Neither am I questioning the Lowells and Tambaughs in our field who are not perfect and make mistakes, such as believing in the existence of canals on Mars. However, I *am* attacking the *dogmatism* with which the Hegels in our business defend the Waterfall as the only true and effective method of developing software, therefore, yielding nothing.

The Waterfall has helped us tame problems that were tameable. But, many of them have already been solved. Now, we are facing more and more wicked problems, where the computer's initial results are partial solutions and where its final results are only part of the solution.

The problems described in this chapter can be boiled down to matters of inflexibility and disutility. In succeeding chapters, I will discuss ways the Waterfall has been changed and other methods that have been developed to make software development adapt to the kinds of problems we need to solve.

Someone once said: "If the only tool you have is a hammer, you tend to see problems in terms of nails." If the only model we have is the Waterfall, then we will see our field in terms of problems that can be solved using it. Our world and our field are richer than that. We need a toolbox full of models.

CHAPTER FIVE
Whirlpools, Incrementals, and Spirals

In this chapter, I will talk about certain variations of the Waterfall that are very important. The last chapter concluded with an illustration of a model actually used to produce software. (See Figure 4-8 in Chapter Four.) It was referred to as a Waterfall by developers who changed it in order to get the project done. As you can see, it is not really a Waterfall. I would describe it more as a Whirlpool.

In addition to Whirlpools, there are other variations invented by major buyers of software, such as NASA and the Department of Defense, and also by investigators in the field, such as Barry Boehm and some of my correspondents who did research into how ADE (Aerospace, Defense, and Engineering) programmers actually do their jobs.

A Whirlpool is a very complex model. It is composed of "clumps" of the phases of the classical Waterfall model, and then the composition of these clumps changes several times as the Whirlpool is being used until all the phases of the Waterfall appear in the Whirlpool. They do not have the same timing relationships to other phases as they do in the Waterfall model, and the timing relationships in each epoch of the Whirlpool are not the same as the timing relationships you have in the succeeding epochs of the Whirlpool model. (See Figure 5-1.)

The illustration shows four major steps, each composed of one or more traditional phases of the Waterfall. The first step is composed of the Initiation and Requirements phases, and is staffed mainly by users. There is much more interaction between the initiators of the project and the staff actually doing the requirements, which is why these two phases have the same timing relationship (where Initiation sits on top of Requirements, not off to one side). As shown in the figure, the "what/how" gap occurs between this step and the next.

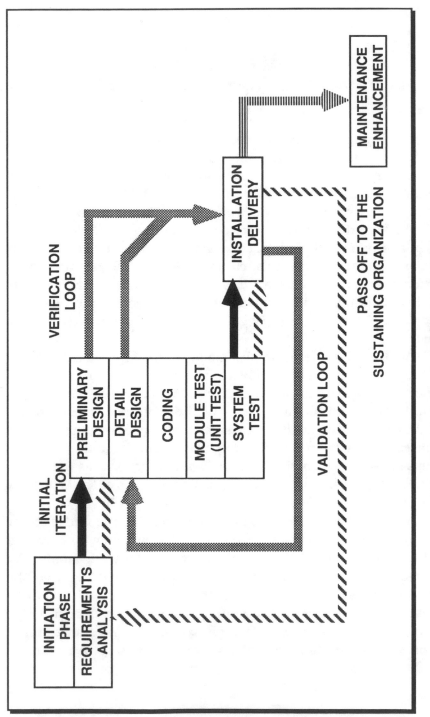

Figure 5-1. The Bastardized Waterfall or Whirlpool

The second major step is composed of the Preliminary Design, Detail Design, Code, and Test phases. The staff here is made up mostly of programmers and analysts. Again, there is much interaction, and the timing of each of these phases is the same.

Yet another gap can be seen between the second and third steps. It seems to be a reverse of the original "what/how" gap: that is, the developers are presenting the new system to the users, rather than the users presenting requirements for a new system to the developers.

The third step is composed of the Installation and Delivery phases, and the last step is composed of the Maintenance and Enhancement phases.

These steps correspond to the simple three-phase Waterfall of Planning, Design, and Implementation mentioned earlier, with Maintenance and Enhancement added.

The first iteration through this series of steps went as expected. At the "what/how" gap, the users tossed the Victorian novel across the gap to the technical staff. They, in turn, worked their way down the phases to the system test.

Now things get interesting. During system test, failures of one type or another were discovered. These came from bugs remaining in the modules, interface problems among the modules, unexpected error conditions (remember the difficulty of getting error-handling code designed correctly the first time in a top-down environment?), requirements and design problems, and "wicked" system characteristics that would be very expensive to correct. All of these problems are the result of the difficulties described in the last chapter.

A second iteration had to be performed. (I call it the verification loop, because it reconciled the new system to the requirements as the developers knew or understood them to be. This is a kind of reverse engineering in that given the system as built, it had to be mapped back into the requirements. This loop also implemented solutions that were not part of the original requirements.

So, the developers moved some activities from the first step into this second "super" step to implement new requirements and to keep costs as low as possible. (See Figure 5-2). Some requirements activities were repeated. The developers moved through the phases of this new super step several times and not always in the same order.

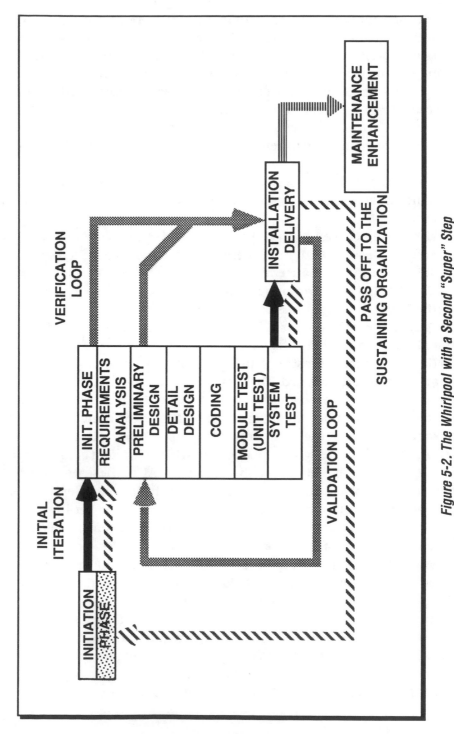

Figure 5-2. The Whirlpool with a Second "Super" Step

Then, in the Installation and Delivery phase, more requirements changes appeared. These occurred because the development took so long and was pushing the outer limits of the budget that management was willing to spend (the business-decision horizon). The kinds of requirements changes that management wanted were the following:

- To truncate the system.

- To curtail interviews with users. (This results in the kind of situation I related previously: "Some time ago, I was in the office of a computing-system user. She had several terminals next to her desk, and would be considered an experienced user. She seemed somewhat distracted, and when I asked, she told me that she had just attended a training session for a new system and it upset her. She concluded that the new system was designed for programmers, not for 'regular' people.")

- To incorporate new requirements that should have appeared in the maintenance and enhancement, but appear now because the original project took so long.

- To incorporate the results of changes in technology, again because the development took so long.

I call this the "Validation Iteration," because the purpose was to reconcile the new system to the expectations of the people who initiated the project, answering the question, "did we build the right system." Again, to save time and money, the developers moved some design and construction steps to the Installation and Delivery step. The model now looks like that shown in Figure 5-3.

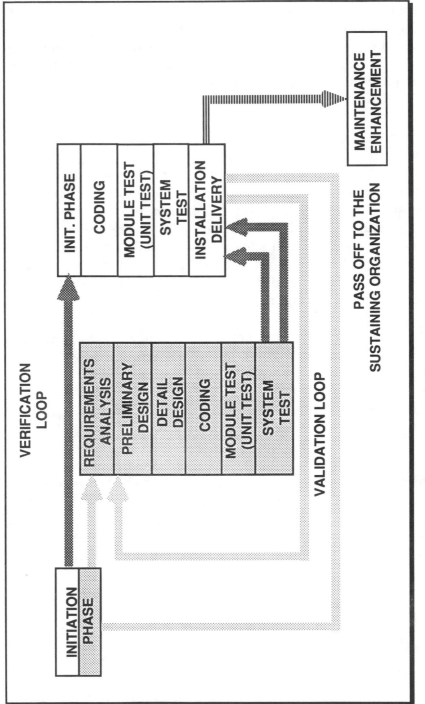

Figure 5-3. Further Modification of the Whirlpool

Notice how the phases of the super steps related to one another as shown in Figures 5-1 through 5-3. There was a lot of interaction among the phases of the super steps. That is why they are drawn coincident in time. The super steps themselves did not remain constant, but were transformed by necessity. Parts of the model were cycled through several times in order to avoid repeating the whole project. They were trying to avoid building it twice. [Brooks 1975]

However, this method of building a system has an important effect on the final step of Maintenance and Enhancement. The final step ought to "look" only at the Installation and Delivery phase, which is the Validation phase, and take its input *only* from that phase. But, Maintenance ends up "looking" at most of the other phases. My correspondent indicated that maintenance programmers had a great deal of difficulty with the system that was passed off to them. They received partial products from the design, coding, testing, and installation steps and *not* the clear, clean, complete, and un-ambiguous system documents from the delivery phase dictated by the Waterfall model.

Of course, the people involved on this project realized that there was some problem with the hand-off and knew what had to be done to improve it. But, by the time they realized what they needed to do, the business decision horizon had been exceeded. Management was worn out, so things were delayed away, and the maintenance activity got off to a shaky start. This is inherent in the Waterfall model itself. It simply takes too long, even though people try to make it more efficient. And, it wears out the management people who are con-stantly explaining how and why they are expending their company's profits.

This Whirlpool is characterized by more iterations than the orthodox model would allow.*And, it was what people *had* to do to be effective and get the job done.

---

*I suspect that there are other transformations made by other software developers who are required to use the Waterfall, and yet are allowed some flexibility. If your version of the Waterfall is different from my descriptions here, please send me your versions so I can add them to my bestiary.

Attenuating and Truncating

Attenuating and truncating is what major buyers do in order to control costs and, at the same time, manage risks. Aside from on-site inspection and demonstrations of software, these buyers depend on documents to gauge their vendor's progress through the Waterfall, and so their strategies for controlling projects involve controlling the documentation. That, in turn, controls the Waterfall. For example, if, for some reason, they do not require a design document, then developers can subside into a code-and-go or some other mode of production.

Less formal methods of doing things do not mean that the activities involved in them are not done. If I do not have to have a verification and validation plan, I am still going to determine if I built the software right and if the right software got built. I just won't write a book about it and I will save a lot of time and trouble, as this book you are reading illustrates.

In the following descriptions, you can assume that the truncating and attenuating are part of the controlling process. Some folks call this a document-driven Waterfall. The Waterfall need not always be document driven or involve much documentation at all; but a special characteristic of it is the formality with which software development is done. This formality is what leads to the voluminous documentation often given as the reason for high cost and long production times.

NASA has an interesting variation based on characterizing software and then performing tasks according to the characterization. This variation is based on NASA Policy NMI 5330.1. This policy categorizes software and establishes planning and documentation practices appropriate to each category.

NASA's variation uses ten scales for measuring aspects of software. The first scale measures how essential is the function of the software. The second measures how acceptable are the failures. The third measures how mature is the software. (In other words, does it involve research, or can it be bought off the shelf?)

The fourth, fifth, and sixth are scales to measure the complexity, size, and the likely cost, respectively. The seventh scale is a measure of the number of organizations that will use the software. (The more using organizations involved, the higher the measure on the scale). The eight, ninth, and tenth scales measure the expected lifetime of the software, the utility of the software, and how tight the development schedule is.

Software that rates high on these scales is classified A. Software that rates low gets a G. The in-between classification is still somewhat subjective. For example, software that performs a critical function and has no tolerance for failure probably rates an A, while code that rates high for having a tight development schedule and will be used by many organizations, but does not rate high on the other scales, would probably rate an F or G. (See Figure 5-4.)

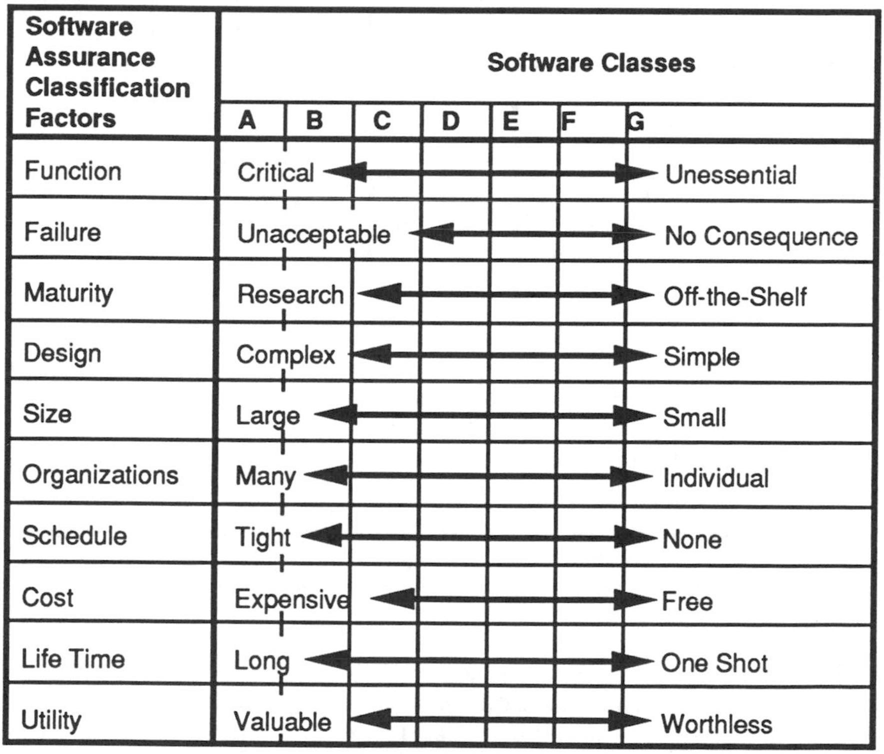

Software Assurance Classification Factors	Software Classes						
	A	B	C	D	E	F	G
Function	Critical ◄──────────────► Unessential						
Failure	Unacceptable ◄────────► No Consequence						
Maturity	Research ◄────────────► Off-the-Shelf						
Design	Complex ◄─────────────► Simple						
Size	Large ◄───────────────► Small						
Organizations	Many ◄────────────────► Individual						
Schedule	Tight ◄───────────────► None						
Cost	Expensive ◄───────────► Free						
Life Time	Long ◄────────────────► One Shot						
Utility	Valuable ◄────────────► Worthless						

Figure 5-4. Software Classification Considerations

At any rate, the classification is entered into the Minimum Software Requirements Matrix. (See Figure 5-5.) As you might expect, software that is rated A gets full treatment from the developers, and you can expect them to implement a full-fledged Waterfall.

G-rated software gets short shrift, and in-between software gets in-between treatment.

Assurance Practices	Software Categories						
	A	B	C	D	E	F	G
Documentation	X	X	X	X	X	X	
Management Plan	X	X	X	X	X		
Assurance Plan	X	X	X	X			
Quality Assurance Plan	X	#	#	#	#		
Independent Verification and Validation Plan	X	X	#	#	#		
Configuration Management Plan	X	X	X	#	#		
Test Plan	X	X	X	#	#		

X = Required
# = Required as a section of the plan indicated directly above as being required (X).

Figure 5-5. Minimum Software Assurance Requirements

Notice that Software Quality Assurance (SQA), also shown in Figure 5-5, is the first assurance practice that gets sacrificed. I think this is a mistake. David Card, et al., show in an article in IEEE Transactions on Software Engineering that one of the determinants of software reliability is Software Quality Assurance. [Card et. al. 1987] One would think that NASA would be very interested in reliability.

The Minimum Software Requirements Matrix shows how the Waterfall can be attenuated as in class D, where SQA, independent verification and validation, configuration management, and test plans are subsumed into the assurance plan. It also illustrates how the Waterfall is truncated, as in class F, where all the plans are eliminated.

The DoD has a similar scheme. DOD-HDBK-287 describes how to tailor the 2167 development procedure: "This Directive [DODD 4120.21] requires all DOD components [organizations, contractors, etc.] to apply military specifications and standards *selectively* and to *tailor* them before use on a contract. Thus, the SAM [Software Acquisition Manager] must tailor DOD-STD-2167 and its related DIDs [Data Item Descriptions, which are the document types] and standards in order to develop and support the system in the most cost-effective manner. ... Tailoring is a process performed many times throughout the life cycle ... Many different events trigger the need to tailor ... First and foremost, tailoring should take place every time the system enters a new life cycle phase (i.e., Concept, Exploration, Demonstration and Validation, Full-Scale Development, and Production and Deployment)." [DOD-HDBK-287, p.32] [**Author's note:** Emphasis added and indicated by italics.]

The DoD scheme is based on a matrix showing the software's category versus the software's use. This matrix is shown in Figure 5-6. Figure 5-7 is an illustration of the tailoring process for software requirements.

The "business" side of the Department of Defense has yet another tailoring procedure. It's a neat idea based on computing what they call a "complexity" number, and is shown in Figure 5-8. [DOD-STD-7935, 1983, pp.2-14] This, then, is cranked into the documentation/complexity chart shown in Figure 5-9. From that, one can figure out what documents to produce, and, by implication, which phases to attenuate or skip completely.

So, as you can see, the Waterfall is modified *unselfconsciously* by developers in an organization in order to get the job done, and *deliberately* as part of a major buyer's attempt to be practical.

Sample of a Completed Software Category
Use Table—From DOD-HDBK-287

	OPERATIONAL	SUPPORT	DIAGNOSTIC
	●	●	●
	●	●	●
	●		

CATEGORY 1 — NEWLY DEVELOPED SOFTWARE TO BE INCLUDED IN A CSCI

CATEGORY 2 — NEWLY DEVELOPED SOFTWARE TO BE INCLUDED IN A HWCI, SYSTEM OR SEGMENT

CATEGORY 3 — NON-DELIVERABLE SOFTWARE USED IN THE DEVELOPMENT ENVIRONMENT

CATEGORY 5 — EXISTING SOFTWARE THAT WILL BE MODIFIED AND USED IN A DELIVERABLE ITEM

CATEGORY 4 — UNMODIFIED SOFTWARE, EITHER COMMERCIALLY AVAILABLE OR REUSABLE, USED IN A DELIVERABLE ITEM

Figure 5-6. Software Category Use Matrix

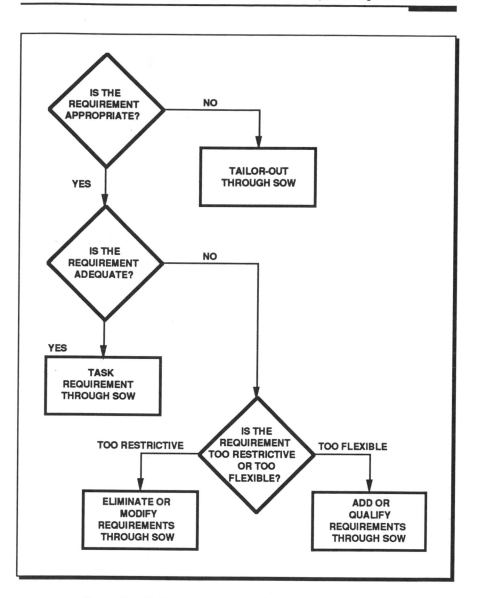

Figure 5-7. Tailoring Process for Software Requirements

COMPLEXITY / FACTORS	1	2	3	4	5
1. ORIGINALITY REQUIRED	NONE: REPROGRAM ON DIFFERENT EQUIPMENT	MINIMUM: MORE STRINGENT REQUIREMENTS	LIMITED: MORE ENVIRONMENT, NEW INTERFACES	CONSIDERABLE: APPLY EXISTING STATE OF ART TO ENVIRONMENT	EXTENSIVE: REQUIRES ADVANCE IN STATE OF THE ART
2. DEGREE OF GENERALITY	HIGHLY RESTRICTED. SINGLE PURPOSE.	RESTRICTED: PARAMETERIZED FOR A RANGE OF CAPABILITIES	LIMITED FLEXIBILITY; ALLOWS SOME CHANGE IN FORMAT	MULTI-PURPOSE; FLEXIBLE FORMAT, RANGE OF SUBJECTS.	VERY FLEXIBLE: ABLE TO HANDLE A BROAD RANGE OF SUBJECT MATTER ON DIFFERENT EQUIPMENT
3. SPAN OF OPERATION	LOCAL OR UTILITY	COMPONENT COMMAND	SINGLE COMMAND	MULTI-COMMAND	DEFENSE DEPARTMENT WORLD-WIDE
4. CHANGE IN SCOPE AND OBJECTIVE	NONE	INFREQUENT	OCCASIONAL	FREQUENT	CONTINUOUS
5. EQUIPMENT COMPLEXITY	SINGLE MACHINE, ROUTINE PROCESSING	SINGLE MACHINE, ROUTINE PROCESSING, EXTENDED PERIPHERAL SYSTEM	MULTI-COMPUTER, STANDARD PERIPHERAL SYSTEM	MULTI-COMPUTER, ADVANCED PROGRAMMING, COMPLEX PERIPHERAL SYSTEM	MASTER CONTROL SYSTEM, MULTI-COMPUTER, AUTO INPUT-OUTPUT AND DISPLAY EQUIPMENT
6. PERSONNEL ASSIGNED	1-2	3-5	5-10	10-18	18 AND OVER
7. DEVELOPMENTAL COST	3-15K	15-70K	70-200K	200-500K	OVER 500K

Figure 5-8. Levels of Project Complexity

FACTORS / COMPLEXITY	1	2	3	4	5
8 CRITICALITY	DATA PROCESSING	ROUTINE OPERATIONS	PERSONNEL SAFETY	UNIT SURVIVAL	NATIONAL DEFENSE
9 AVERAGE RESPONSE TIME TO PROGRAM CHANGES	2 OR MORE WEEKS	1-2 WEEKS	3-7 DAYS	1-3 DAYS	1-24 HOURS
10 AVERAGE RESPONSE TIME TO DATA INPUTS	2 OR MORE WEEKS	1-2 WEEKS	1-7 DAYS	1-24 HOURS	9-60 MINUTES
11 PROGRAMMING LANGUAGES	HIGH LEVEL LANGUAGE	HIGH LEVEL AND LIMITED ASSEMBLY LANGUAGE	HIGH LEVEL AND EXTENSIVE ASSEMBLY LANGUAGE	ASSEMBLY LANGUAGE	MACHINE LANGUAGE
12 CONCURRENT SOFTWARE DEVELOPMENT	NONE	LIMITED	MODERATE	EXTENSIVE	EXHAUSTIVE
TOTALS	*1*	*2*	*3*	*4*	*5*
					COMPLEXITY TOTAL:

From DOD-STD-7935, 15 February 1983

Figure 5-8. Levels of Project Complexity (cont.)

111

Complexity Total	Document Types					
12 - 15			UM			
12 - 26			UM OM MM	PT		
24 - 38	FD		UM OM MM	PT		
36 - 50	FD	SS	UM OM MM	PT	RT	
48 - 60	FD	SS PS	UM OM MM	PT	RT	

Notes:

1. Preparation of the Data Requirements Document, the Data Base Specification, and the Implementation Procedures is situationally dependent.

2. Additional document types may be required at lower complexities.

Abbreviations:

FD-Functional Description   OM-Computer Operation Manual
SS-System/Subsystem Specs.   MM-Program Maintenance Manual
PS-Program Specification   PT-Test Plan
UM-User's Manual   RT-Test Analysis Reports

Figure 5-9. Document Types/Project Complexity

Incrementals

Another way to control the Waterfall is to perform it in sections. This is popularly known as *incremental development*. The two most important Incremental models are Barry Boehm's version and a version from one of my correspondents at Boeing.

In Boehm's version, shown in Figure 5-10, the Waterfall proceeds as usual through completion of the Preliminary Design phase. Then, several mini-projects are undertaken, each with the goal of implementing some of the requirements. The system is complete after the last mini-project is complete. However, there is useful functionality before that time.

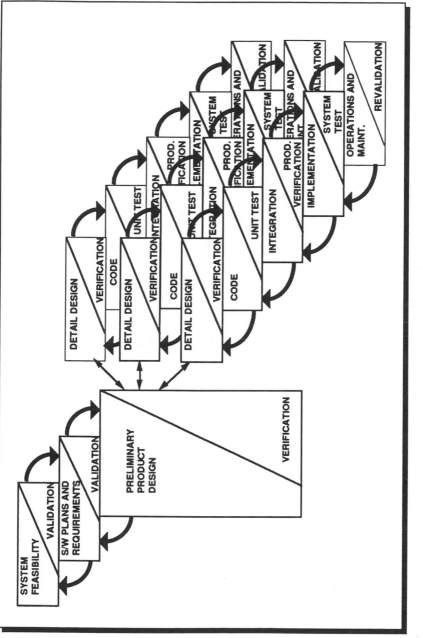

Figure 5-10. Boehm's Incremental Model

113

Maintaining clean interfaces among the modules in the system is critical in decomposing the system into sub-projects. This is because some modules will be completed long before other modules with which they will interface. This model is based on a "complete" set of requirements, which, as I have previously shown, is problematic.

Boeing's version [Gilchrist, et al 1989], shown in Figure 5-11, was developed after observing how Aerospace, Defense, and Engineering (ADE) programmers actually did their jobs. It is similar to Barry Boehm's, but with one important difference. It does not depend on a complete set of requirements, but starts with general objectives, and proceeds by translating some of those objectives into requirements and then implementing them. The cycle then repeats. Starting the development process with general objectives rather than with a complete set of requirements is important, because it allows requirements to adjust to changing conditions. When the requirements and the design are closely related in time, the "what/how" gap is significantly reduced in size.

This is a simplified description of the Incremental Development model, but it is accurate as far as it goes. The people who developed it assure me that much much more is actually done, but I suspect they feel a little guilty about simplifying the orthodox Waterfall so it remains unofficial.

Another way of looking at Boeing's Incremental model is as a spiral, shown in Figure 5-12. In a Spiral model, the starting center point represents the resources that are needed to begin the project. As the project proceeds and the spiral forms, the system's growth is represented by changes in the diameter of the spiral. The resources used are measured by the distances between adjoining sections of the line.

An advantage of the Spiral model is that resources remain constant after the project has started up, but the size of the system is growing. This is good news for both management and for the engineering organizations that are asking for the applications. Costs are relatively constant, and the users are quickly getting a return on their investment. In this system, you have good control over the size and cost. And, up to some limit, the more resources you add the faster the system grows. It is a good method that was developed unselfconsciously, again in order to get the job done.

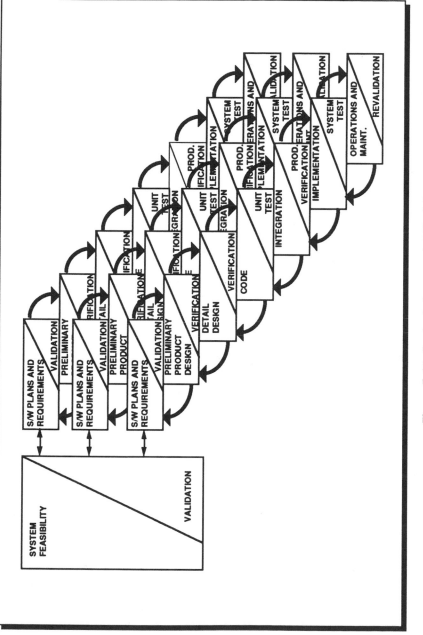

Figure 5-11. Boeing's Incremental Model

115

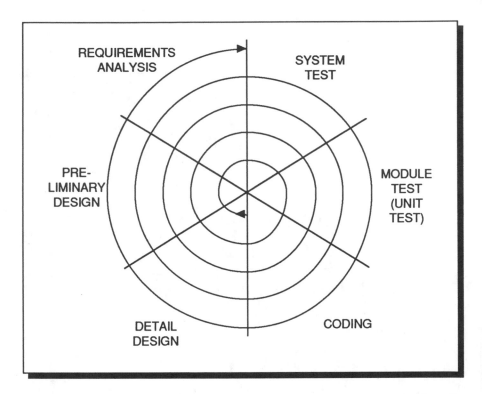

Figure 5-12. Boeing Incremental System Development (Expressed as a Spiral)

Barry Boehm has another Spiral. [Agresti 1986] But, in his Spiral, he introduces another model—Prototyping. (See Figure 5-13.) We will talk more about this in the next chapter, but notice here how that model uses Prototyping to manage costs early on in the project. The Waterfall is used last, and expands resources noticeably. In this way, his model helps to manage risks by keeping costs relatively low early on, and then allocating more resources as the risk becomes lower.

Boehm's model has become quite popular among ADE specialists, and is not so familiar among business developers. If you unroll it, it is similar to the System Development Life Cycle (SDLC) of the procedure 2167 (reviewed in icon form in Figure 5-14). It is particularly useful in ADE projects, because they are risky in nature. Business projects are more conservative. They tend to use mature technology and to work well-known problems.

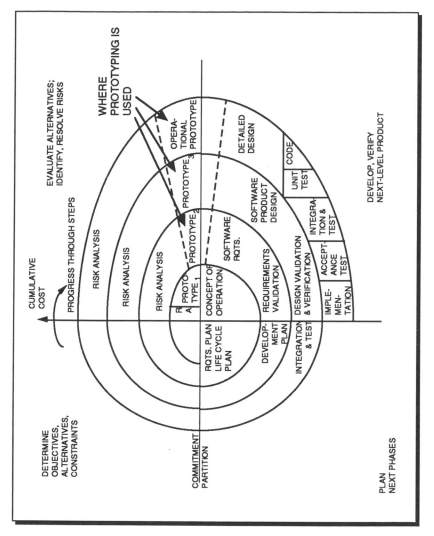

Figure 5-13. Boehm's Spiral Model

117

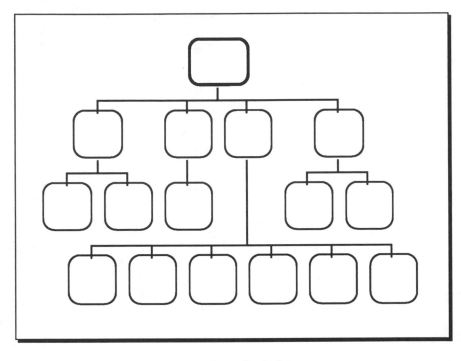

Figure 5-14. DOD SLC Icon

I believe the Spiral model actually is applicable to many business applications, especially those for which success is not guaranteed or the applications require much computation, such as in decision support systems.

Other applications for the Spiral are Material and Resource Planning problems. These are risky problems because they are so difficult to implement, are very, very large, have many human interactions, and involve many processes performed by humans. The waste of years of effort using the traditional Waterfall might be avoided if another, quicker method could be applied early in the project to get stronger indicators of likely success. Developers could use a breadboard, mockup, or prototype, and these will be discussed next.

CHAPTER SIX
Prototyping

The Greco-Roman period in western culture was one of the glorious peaks of civilization in human history. After it waned, there followed the Age of Faith, which was a wide and deep valley. At the far edge of the valley arose another peak—our modern world.

Some people mark the beginning of the modern period at the Renaissance. The famous painter and sculptor, Michelangelo, lived then. His was a tortured soul, struggling with the perfect expression of faith in a time of rapid change. He produced many famous works, such as the painting of the Sistine chapel, and sculptures such as the Pietà, David, and the Medici tombs in Florence, among other works.

There is a peculiar feature about David and the figure of Dawn in the work at the Medici tombs. If you look at the photo of the right hand of David and our sketch of the hand of Dawn, you will see that they look suspiciously alike. (See Figures 6-1 and 6-2.) Well, they are, and for a very good reason. You see, Michelangelo used terra cotta figures of various parts of the anatomy as *models* to aid him in composition, to speed his work, and to transfer good design features. (See Figure 6-3.)

Figure 6-1. The Right Hand of Michelangelo's David (photo by David Finn)

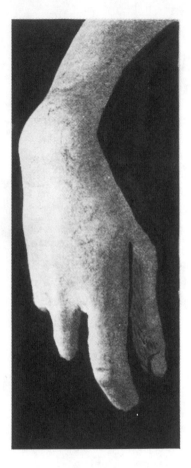

Figure 6-2. Sketch of the Right Hand of Michelangelo's Dawn

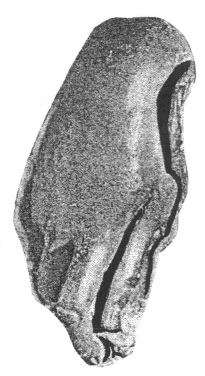

Figure 6-3. Sketch of Michelangelo's Terra Cotta Model of a Right Hand

Using and reusing models was very popular even back then. Ludwig Goldscheider, in his book entitled *A Survey of Michelangelo's Models in Wax and Clay*, quotes other authors about the purpose of small models:

" 'When sculptors wish to work on a marble statue they usually make first what they call "a model" for it, which is a guide pattern (esempio), about half a *braccio* high (a little under twelve inches), sometimes less or more, just as it suits them; and they make it in clay, or wax, or stucco. Such a model shows, in accordance with the dimensions of the block quarried for the statue, the attitude and the proportions of the figure.' '... For all his works Michelangelo always made models, but he rectified [his drawings after them] from nature while he proceeded with his work.'

"... Michelangelo made each small model for a special statue, but often used it again for figures in a painting, or in a drawing, or for a different sculpture." [Goldscheider 1962]

Figure 6-4 shows a detail of the right-side of the statue of David, and Figure 6-5 shows a detail of a wax model of David from the same view. Though tiny, this model was incredibly thorough and detailed. (See Figure 6-6.)

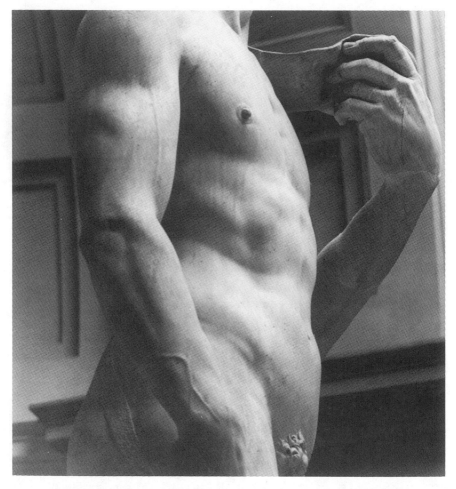

Figure 6-4. Detail of the Statue of David from One-Quarter Right
(photo by David Finn)

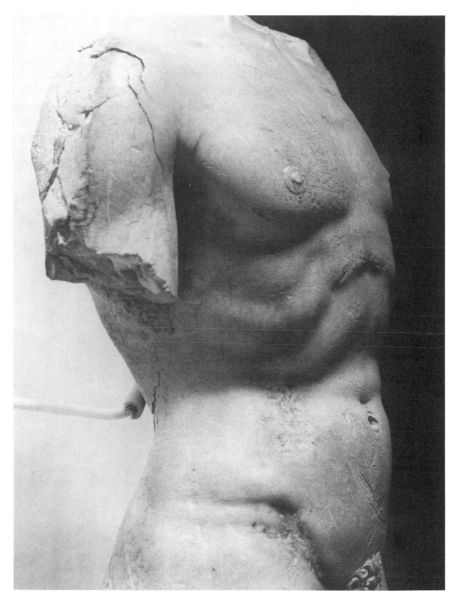

Figure 6-5. Detail of the Model of David from One-Quarter Right
(photo by David Finn)

Figure 6-6. The Model of David (shown next to photographer David Finn's hand to indicate size)

These models in wax, clay, and terra cotta were *prototypes*, but not exactly in the same sense as what many of us mean when we talk about software prototypes.

Small-scale models are also used in advertising. During the last century, exquisitely made ship models were used to entice investors. These were not used to actually build ships; other devices were used for that. But these models were very successful, and many thousands were built. They became popular items in home decoration, and several museums today are devoted exclusively to them.

One of the most well known models of our century is that of DNA, shown many thousands of times larger than the molecule it represents. The DNA model is used as an aid to understanding the relationships among the bases of the DNA molecule—the genetic code. It is a window looking out onto the structure of life itself.

There are many kinds of models in the hardware world. Some are full-scale models having the same size as what is being modeled; but made of different, usually inexpensive, materials. These models, called mockups, are used for examining the size relationships between the model and other things in the real world. An example of a mockup is a cardboard model used to test a driver's field of vision in a new automobile.

Small-scale models of large things are often built to inexpensively test the forces that the full-scale version is likely to encounter. An example is a wind tunnel model.

Large-scale models of very small things are often used to learn about and study structures that would otherwise be difficult or sometimes even impossible to study. The components of integrated circuits are laid out on very large, wall-sized surfaces so the designers will have access to them. Then, the entire surface is reduced in size until it takes up an area of about one-quarter inch.

Electronics has two common models: breadboards and brassboards. The term *breadboard* comes from the days when electronic circuits, composed of discreet and large components, were built-up on surfaces that looked like and sometimes actually were breadboards or other such informal surfaces. These allowed for fast, convenient construction and easy access to the parts. Breadboards usually are not fully functional, but are used only for experimental or exploratory purposes.

Brassboards are fully functional versions of the circuits built up on breadboards. They often do not have the same performance characteristics as the final product will, because the construction techniques used on them affect the characteristics. However, they look very much like the final product, and are usually about the same shape and weight with the same types of components. They are prototypes.

In the hardware world, a *prototype* is usually a fully functional, full-scale version of the final product. The prototype is often painstakingly built without the aid of the production tools that are used later in full production, and with workers who are not yet perfecting their skills by producing many copies of the product. It is intended that many copies of this product will eventually be produced in roughly the same way as the prototype, but they will make use of an array of manufacturing aids that come into play during full-scale production.

There are many views of prototyping in the software world, but I propose the one used by William Agresti because he uses the notion of a "model" as it is used in engineering: "… Prototyping is the process of building a working *model* of a system." [Emphasis added.] He goes on: "It is a familiar practice in engineering, to obtain an early version of a product or system. Engineering prototypes can vary in size (scaled down or full size) and functionality (limited capability or a complete set of functions). In any case, the objective of prototyping is to clarify the characteristics and operation of a product or system by constructing a version that can be exercised. [Agresti 1986. *What Are the New Paradigms?*]

How Prototyping is Used

Prototyping begins with some type of proto-system. This proto-system could be embedded in a fourth-generation language's syntax, and internal and external functions. It is often used with a database, a query language supported by the 4GL, screen and report generators (if they are not already part of the 4GL or database), and access to data that will be processed by the system.

The proto-system could be embedded in one or more collections of functions, such as libraries of object or source code. Or, it could be an already existing system that is being used as a model.

A proto-system can come from partial solutions. Suppose your problem is that you are trying to analyze how sand dunes move through a desert to help you understand aridity. One of the things you can do is build a partial solution. First, understand how individual grains move, and then scale up, adding in forces such as gravity, which may have been swamped by electrical forces at the smaller scale.

Prototypes can come from prototyping programs. For example, Prototyper, for the Macintosh, by Smithers and Barnes, helps you to prototype the user interface for programs on the Macintosh. This program enables you to build up the interface of an application very quickly. The program then puts out the code that represents the interface you prototyped. The code has within it a place to add your application-specific code to complete the development process. All along, the prototype can be exercised to test development.

Prototypes can come from the operation of simulation programs. Foresight, from Athena Systems, is an example. Using this system, the developer can create a model of a system on the screen; a cockpit, for example. The users exercise the model and the system produces outputs that can be used in final design of the program.

Finally, prototypes can come from your colleagues desk drawers and from sample programs and algorithms you find in journals, libraries, and government publications.

Then, you get some sort of requirements list. Sometimes it is quite informal, of the type used in the code-and-go shops. If the program is for yourself, you might start with just an idea in your head with nothing written down. If it is for your customer, the requirements could arrive in some sort of memo.

Next, you transform the requirements into a working model by changing or operating your proto-system to include them. With a 4GL, you transform the requirements into language and macro commands.

With libraries, you write a "driver," the top level program, and select and insert calls to the library functions that represent the requirements. Then, you integrate them by writing code to handle input, output, error processing functions, operator messages, and connections between functions.

With an existing system, you locate and make changes to the places that reflect the requirements.

In any case, you then compile or recompile until no syntactic errors are detected and do whatever verification procedure is indicated. Next, you show the results to the customer or decide (if *you* are the customer) whether it is doing what you want. If new requirements emerge, repeat the process.

If no more changes are indicated, then you do the documentation unless somebody has already been doing it in parallel. The documentation includes the user's and programmer's manuals. The programmer's manual should contain any requirements that were recorded, any design data, context diagrams, call trees, and test cases. Then, clean up the code by adding comments where appropriate, tightening up the code, etc. Finally, shrink-wrap and ship it.

The toughest system to get started is an existing one, because most of the time you're going to have to *learn* it first and it is almost certain that it will need to have the code "cleaned up." In other words, it is probably spaghetti code. Code restructurers could be an aid here in preparing a good starting point.

You will find that much less documentation is required with prototyping than with the Waterfall because you end up with the *right* documentation. You tend to write about the one thing that was produced rather than each of the variations (which get 'written up' and sent back and forth between the developers and users).

When and Where Prototyping is Used

The above is a simplified description that shows prototyping used to develop an end product. In this description, prototyping was a development method in its own right replacing another method like the Waterfall. But, there are various other uses for prototyping in association with the Waterfall and I will discuss these next.

Prototyping outside the Waterfall is shown in Barry Boehm's Spiral model (shown in Figure 6-7). Here, he shows a prototyping step followed by the Waterfall model. The System Development Life Cycle (SDLC) of the Department of Defense (shown in Figure 6-8) also shows prototyping occurring as a separate step early on, followed by a "full-scale" production Waterfall model. These models may look different, but they are really very similar.

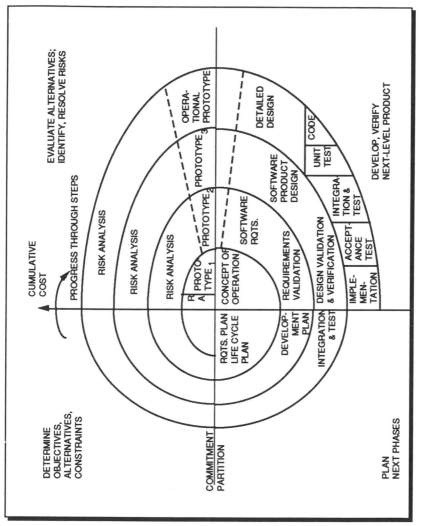

Figure 6-7. Barry Boehm's Spiral Model

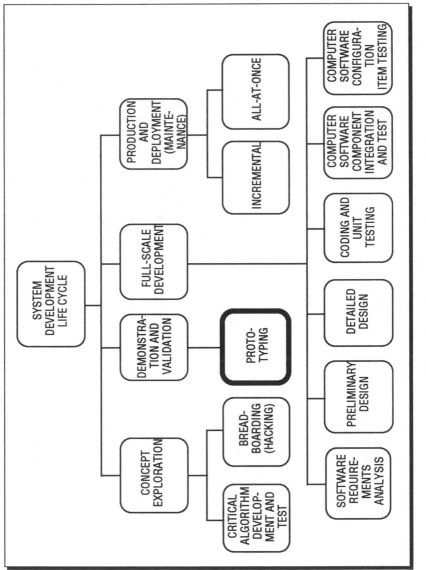

Figure 6-8. The System Development Life Cycle of the DoD

130

The purpose here is to limit risk. Very often, software development is risky, as in developing applications around extremely complex new algorithms for mathematical analyses. Sometimes, it is associated with high risk, new hardware technology such as SDI. The objective here is to get a preliminary indication of whether or not the new technology can be made to work *before* making heavy investments in resources. These models are referred to as "risk driven." Prototyping is also used in maintenance and enhancement as a way of producing rapid changes to correct serious flaws in the design, such as changing algorithms to obtain the desired results.

Prototyping Partially Replacing the Waterfall Model

Many other applications are based on proven, mature technology, but they are developed in an environment in which getting the requirements is very difficult. This often happens in large enterprises that have in-house programming organizations and are accustomed to having custom systems built. In this type of environment, for many reasons the needs and wants of the users are difficult to obtain. Users, who have given their requirements to the development team, need some feedback about the system to clarify their needs. So, portions of the software to be encountered by them are modeled as "mockups" and presented to them for approval and/or change.

Every once in a while, a bright soul might watch the users try to use the system, note the good and bad points of the mockup, and use this information to build another, easier to use, version. In any event, the Waterfall process then proceeds as before, with only the requirements-gathering step partially or completely replaced. (See Figure 6-9.)

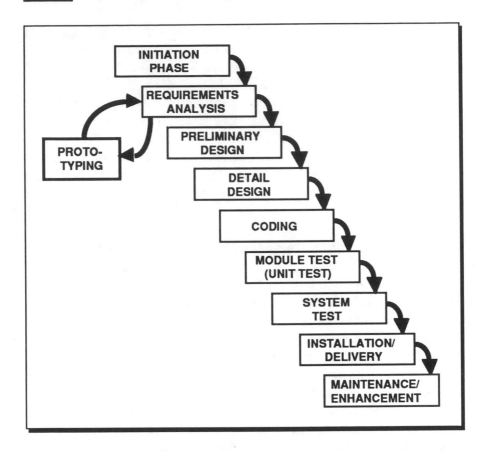

Figure 6-9. Prototyping Partially or Completely Replacing the Requirements Phase

NASA's Waterfall includes prototyping in parallel with the first few steps. Their reasons are similar to those the DoD and Boehm use, but prototyping is done within the Waterfall itself. (See Figure 6-10.)

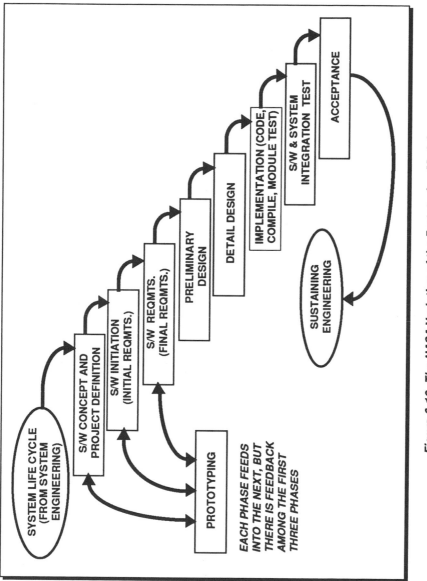

Figure 6-10. *The NASA Variation of the Prototyping Model*

EACH PHASE FEEDS INTO THE NEXT, BUT THERE IS FEEDBACK AMONG THE FIRST THREE PHASES

133

Prototyping Fully Replacing the Waterfall Model

But, prototyping is also an alternative to the Waterfall model; it can completely replace it. There are several approaches. The first, which I call Basic Prototyping, is a procedure similar to the one I described above. A second approach is called Operational Specification. This is combined with a Transformational Implementation to complete the development process.

A good description of Basic Prototyping was given by Kenneth Lantz. His model consists of a number of steps as shown in Figure 6-11. [Lantz 1986] As in the Waterfall model, time is represented moving from left to right, and the steps have time relationships to one another. It starts with determining feasibility, followed by a study of the present system. Then, there are four steps that overlap:

1. Define the prototype.
2. Build the prototype.
3. Execute the prototype.
4. Convert the system.

The last step is to install the system, creating seven steps in all.

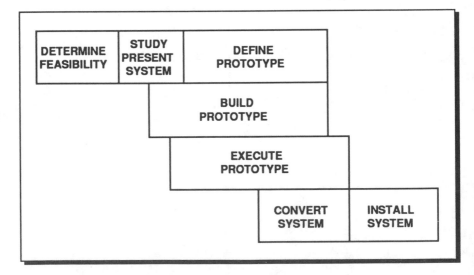

Figure 6-11. The Basic Prototyping Model

The time-coincident relationships among the four steps represent iterations, if you will, but not in a strict sense. It is not a case of starting at step A, followed by B, then C, and finally step D, and then repeating step A, followed by B, etc., etc., in strict order. It is more a case that the steps are performed in a sequence that makes sense in the *context* in which they are performed.

For example, building and exercising the prototype can occur repeatedly before further definition of the system needs to be done. Sometimes, these steps can occur in parallel, where testing is going on while requirements are being developed. As a matter of fact, since the user is constantly exercising the prototype, he is constantly in a position to revise the requirements. In addition, he is constantly testing the system and, in that way, is always doing some acceptance testing on it.

For Lantz, prototyping is a way of producing the system from beginning to end. This might be hard to accept for those of you who are Waterfall advocates, but it is not so different from the objectives you are accustomed to. There are requirements, designs, builds, and tests. The process does proceed in about the order listed. But, every step along the way provides feedback to previous steps. And, here is what is so different about prototyping: every step along the way has, as part of it, elements from every other step.

As a matter of fact, this does happen using the Waterfall. Marvin Zelkowitz reports that 34% of design activity occurs during the Coding phase, more than 10% during the Integration Test phase, 6% during the Acceptance Test phase, and only 50% of the design is done during the Design phase of a Waterfall. (He did not include a Requirements phase in his study.) [Zeklowitz 1988, pp.331, 336]

The second replacement method is a two-step approach. The first step is called an Operational Specification and the second is called a Transformational Implementation. The first step produces a formal specification for software that will satisfy the user. The second step transforms the specification into the finished product.

As Agresti observes in the introduction to Part IV, *Operational Specification*, from the New Paradigms for Software Development tutorial: The objective of the Operational approach is to "... exhibit the behavior of the proposed software system ..." early on. This is because it "... is expressed in a language or form that allows it to be evaluated or interpreted to show system behavior." This is useful because, as Agresti observes, "... users and developers must wait well into the design phase before they have objects (e.g., modules or procedures) that are producing system behavior." [Agresti 1986]

In addition, this new approach provides a better conceptual model for the user. This makes it easier for the user to provide requirements and to accept the final version, because the conceptual model gives them the ability to predict at least some of the results from operating the system.

"The conventional approach places great emphasis on separating requirements (external behavior) from internal structure ... the design phase [of the conventional approach] provides the high level mechanism that will produce the required behavior but those structures must also fit the implementation environment and meet performance constraints. ... [it] separates high-level (intermodule) mechanisms, which are determined during design, from low-level (intramodule) mechanisms, which are determined during imple-mentation. ... [The] intramodule mechanisms are interleaved with implementation-language decisions."

The Operational approach "freely interleaves requirements and internal structure, [but] separates problem-oriented structure from implementation considerations. ... All functional mechanisms [, not just the high level ones,] have been chosen by the time the opera-tional specification is complete [and it] separates mechanisms from their realizations in terms of implementation language." [Zave 1986]

This can all be a bit confusing, so I will give an example contrasting the Waterfall with the operational specification. In the example, the Waterfall is applied to a magazine subscription system and the operational specification approach to a public library system. The subscription problem is a real-life example from Barry Boehm's book, *Software Engineering Economics*. [Boehm 1981, p.3] The public library example is a hypothetical case appearing in an article by John Cameron. [Cameron 1986]

In the examples, it was important for both organizations to minimize costs and optimize performance. And, to accomplish this, it was necessary to automate both existing systems.

Admittedly, the Cameron article has a shortcoming because it is not based on the real world. And, the magazine publisher in the Boehm subscription case also needs to optimize revenues and profits, where the public library has no such motivation. However, both also have similar cultural goals including being an information transfer service, which implies that their processes are generally similar.

In Boehm's subscription case, an early effort proved unsuccessful. The development involved top-down, stepwise refinement: the Waterfall. The context diagram at the top level consisted of input, process, and output. The next level showed process decomposed into checking valid input, processing valid input to produce a transaction file and, finally, generating the outputs. The input validity checking was further decomposed into determining data type, checking versus validity criteria, and checking versus authorization code. (See Figure 6-12.)

It yielded a solution in which:

" • Costs went up
 • Reliability and quality of service went down
 • More clerical people were required
 • Employee morale went down
 • Employee turnover went up" [Boehm 1981, p.6]

Some of these results were caused by not being able to locate input errors early enough in the processing to correct them without significant cost, increased control, and delay. An example of such an error was the renewal of nonexistent subscriptions.

The story has a happy ending, however. The magazine hired a person who took a slightly different approach, asked some important questions, found answers, and still used a top-down approach but came up with a different solution. It yielded the following:

" • The number of clerical workers was reduced from over 40 to fewer than 20.

 • Clerical errors were reduced to a small fraction of the 'subscriber errors' (for example, duplicate orders or payments).

 • Virtually all transactions were handled in less than a week, compared to frequent delays of over a month in the previous system.

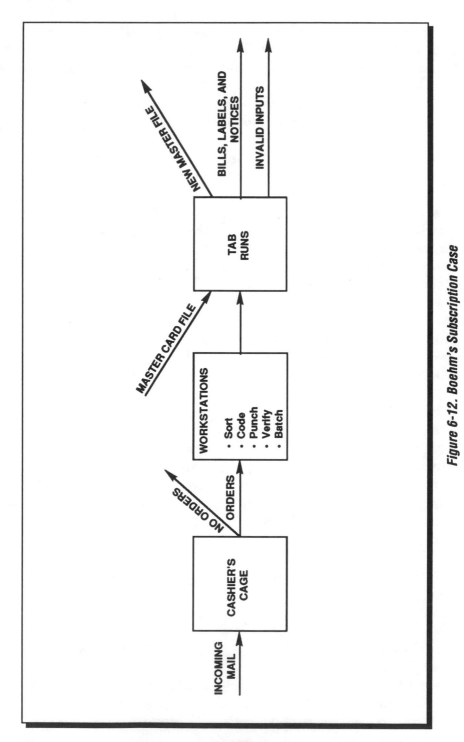

Figure 6-12. Boehm's Subscription Case

- The new system was handling a 33 percent increase in workload.

- Subjective responses from the clerks indicated an increased feeling of job satisfaction. The single-step order entry gave them a more meaningful job to perform, with more opportunity to exercise their own judgment in handling problems and exceptions." [Boehm 1981, p.8]

Boehm claims that the approach, which he calls the Economic Programming approach, made the success possible. This approach involves determining the objectives of the organization, what decisions must be made to affect these objectives, what constrains the range of choices, what evaluation criteria there are, and what is the decision that results in the optimum outcome.

I am sure that the different approach had something to do with the ultimate success of the project. But, notice that it was a system, as Brooks observes, that had to be built twice. [Brooks 1975, p.116] The developers of the second system *must* have been aware of the deficiencies of the previous system and learned something from it. Notice also that the main problem with the first system was error detection and correction.

The library example, on the other hand, started by building a model of the current system. The developers might very well have asked similar initial questions like those asked by the successful developer of the *second* system in the subscription example. But, in addition, they modeled the processes of the system. They asked "what are the processes, what activities compose them, what other processes are there, and how do they combine to form a network (an enterprise model, if you will)?"

One of the processes the developer would model would be the "book" process. (See Figure 6-13.) He would determine that it is composed of six activities: Acquiring the books, classifying the books, lending out the books, renewing the book loans, returning the books, and selling the books. Each of these activities is further classified either as a sequence, iteration, or selection activity. All are arranged on a tree in the order in which the actions can happen. In this scenario, the diagram describes a set of actions that can happen to a book and, by implication, describes what *cannot* happen: a LEND cannot immediately follow an ACQUIRE, a SELL cannot immediately follow a LEND or, *in the case of Boehm's subscription example, a subscription renewal cannot exist before a subscription activity has taken place.* If an input suggests that a book has been SOLD immediately after a LEND, we know that there has been some error on input because, in accepting this diagram [as a model of our library], we are agreeing that a SELL cannot follow a LEND without an intervening RETURN.

Using this method, we can spot the errors that stymied the first developers in the previous example and very possibly could have prevented the second development from being needed.

The developers and users together build the model, both get feedback early, and the model using JSD notation produced a formal specification that can be reinterpreted to the users by the analysts. It can also serve as input to a method for transforming the specification into a finished program, the Transformational Implementation.

This is not as simple as it might sound. It is not simply a matter of building a translator to change the specification into, say, COBOL. You see, the Operational Specification is independent of all implementation issues, such as the hardware platform and implementation language. It concentrated on building the model of the system to be automated. All the implementation issues must now be considered: the platform, language, timing, capacity, and throughput. In addition, all the optimization features must be considered here.

Much of the thinking and research in the Transformation Implementation is based on using "formal" specifications and applying formal rules to them to transform them into a finished product.

There are many ways of proceeding from the formal specification to the final product, but they are all characterized by automating the steps. In this sense, code generators and fourth-generation languages are included in the basic notion.

Another approach is applying expert system technology to the transformation process. I would expect these aids to help developers rather than replace them. Here are some places where they could be used:

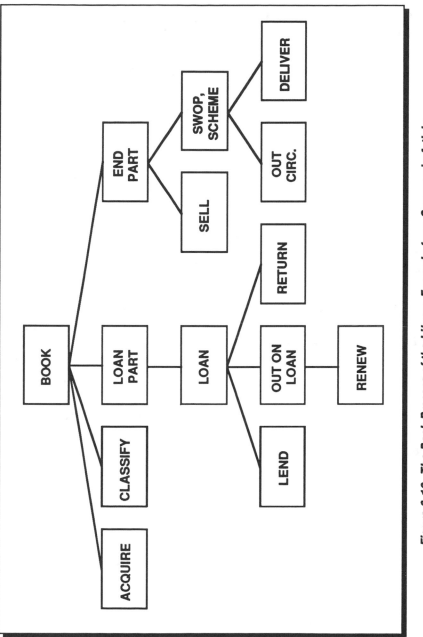

Figure 6-13. The Book Process of the Library Example from Cameron's Article

- Aiding developers in creating a program structure from data flow analysis.

- Converting a program from one language to another.

- Converting a program from one vendor's language implementation to another.

- Auditing complete programs, including an enterprise's entire inventory and producing a set of recommendations for improving the quality of the software under study.

- Producing optimization strategies.

The complete job of transforming a program specification into a finished product cannot be done yet. This part of the field is not yet mature enough in my opinion. However, interesting work is being done in the field. A good description of it is found in Part V of Agresti's tutorial, *New Paradigms for Software Development.* As it matures, it will be a replacement for the Waterfall. The following three diagrams show these approaches: Figure 6-14 shows the Operational Specification process, Figure 6-15 shows the Transformational Implementation, and Figure 6-16 shows them connected together.

In summary, the Operational Specification is a partial replacement of the Waterfall but, together with the Transformational Implementation, it is a prototyping technique and a replacement of the Waterfall model. It improves the process of perfecting requirements by helping to spot errors early on and by giving users good conceptual models of the system they will inherit. These specifications represent the system completely and formally and can then be transformed into the application, which is the final system. Finally, this method is to be used for new, original development.

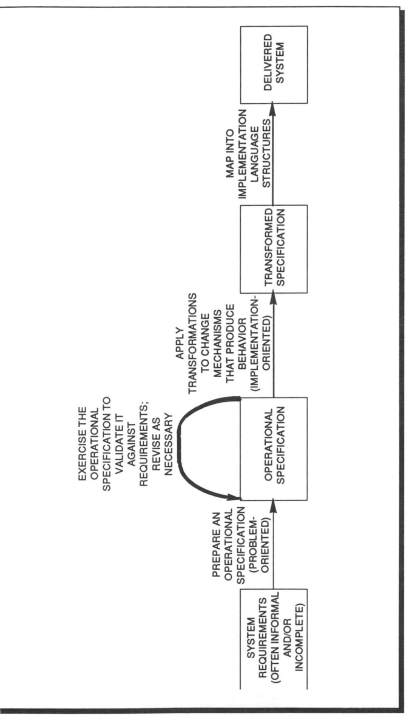

Figure 6-14. The Operational Specification Paradigm

143

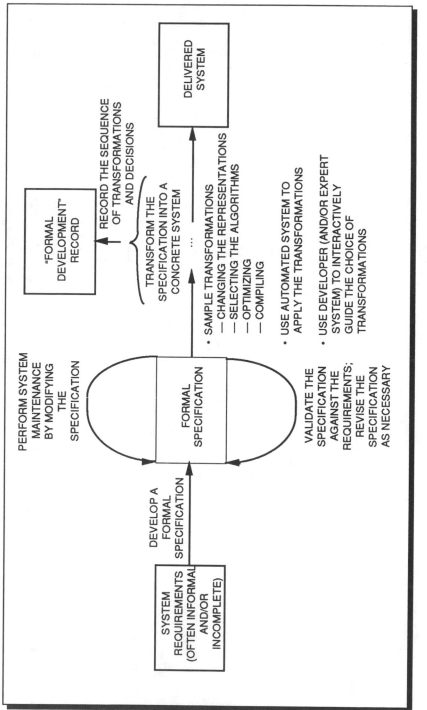

Figure 6-15. The Transformational Implementation Paradigm

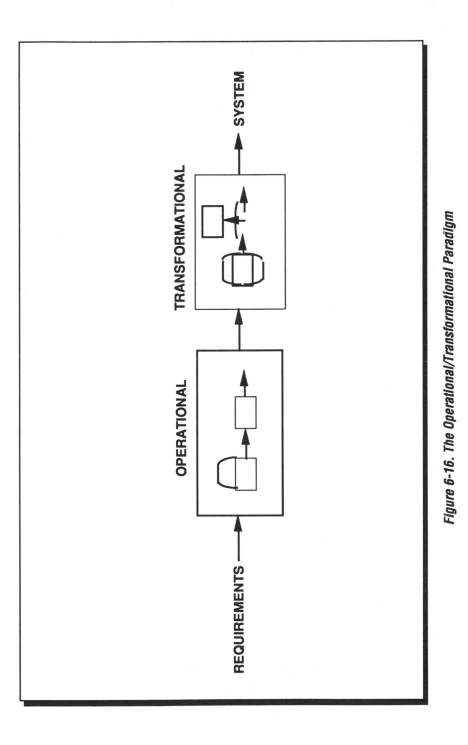

Figure 6-16. The Operational/Transformational Paradigm

The Benefits of Using Prototyping

Many benefits can be claimed for prototyping. It is seen by some as being able to solve, or at least ameliorate, all of the problems of the Waterfall model. It helps to reduce the cost and time to develop software, it improves communication between developers and users, and it improves communication among developers themselves. It bridges the "what/how" gap, sometimes removing it altogether, by allowing the "whats" and the "hows" to freely interleave as in the Operational Specification approach. And, it helps to detect errors early on when something inexpensive can be done about them.

Prototyping is useful for "wicked" problems because it can introduce a partial solution into the environment and stimulate further requirements based on the partial solution's effect. It brings computing back to a human scale. The developer has greater control over the problem; he isn't enmeshed in a process that controls him. And, the user sees that there are quick results again. He is drawn back, willingly, into the process. One of my correspondents reiterated several times how interested the users became, and felt that their interest was key in his successful project.

There are excellent claims in support of the Prototyping model and many of them are probably true. However, there is not much empirical evidence comparing prototyping with the Waterfall model.

One interesting article appeared in the IEEE Transactions on Software Engineering. [Boehm, Gray, and Seewaldt 1984] In the experiment, seven teams developed versions of the same application. It was an interactive version of Barry Boehm's COCOMO model for software cost estimation (containing about 3,000 source lines).

Three of the teams used a prototyping approach, while the other four teams used what the experimenters called the specifying approach (actually, the Waterfall model). They all produced roughly the same product with about the same performance. However, the prototypers produced smaller products, used 40% less code, and expended 45% less effort. Their overall productivity was about the same and the development effort was roughly proportional to the product's size. The prototyped products rated lower in functionality and tolerance of erroneous input, but rated higher in ease of learning and use.

Significantly, the prototyped products rated remarkably higher in maintainability, which appears to be contrary to the notion that prototyped products are harder to maintain and that Waterfall products are easier to maintain.

The distribution of effort was significant. Prototypers spent less time on designing and programming and more on testing, reviewing, and fixing. This supports many of the claims above about the user-oriented effort that results in better perceived communications, happier users, users with better conceptual models, and products that have been tested more.

However, there is a down side. Prototypers produced less documentation and spent less time on it, proportionately, than did the specifiers. And, they produced a less coherent design. These factors are significant, especially since their products were rated lower in extensibility.

Nevertheless, prototyping produced a smaller product of equivalent performance using less effort. The productivity, measured in user satisfaction per manhour, was superior. The interfaces were better, they always had something that was "working," and the deadline effect was reduced. I believe these conclusions are consistent with many of the above claims.

This was a small test involving a small application. We should be cautious about generalizing from this data. However, it is one data point that is consistent with the claims for the technique.

Problems With Prototyping

Prototyping has a bad reputation among more conservative practitioners. One popular notion is that prototyping is just a "quick and dirty" version of the software that will ultimately be developed and is used to perfect requirements. There is a feeling here that the prototype is somehow "unofficial"—that it is just barely authorized; better to be kept out of sight to avoid any embarrassing questions from the keepers of the faith.

There is an erroneous impression that prototyping produces a different *kind* of code than the kind that falls out of the Waterfall model. This is of course a mistake. There is no difference in kind among codes produced through the Waterfall model or through prototyping or with any other method for that matter. This is not to say that there is not "good" code and "bad" code—only that code is code.

Because there is no essential difference between the prototype and the product, the former can become the latter. There might be some implementation issues that might preclude this from being generally true now, but these should fade as our prototyping materials improve.

Prototyping also suffers from bad documentation. Remember the report about the indicators of reliable code being reviews, SQA, and documentation? [Card, et al. 1987] Remember the experiment described above, where less documentation was produced and less time spent on what was produced? Let us look at Figure 6-17.

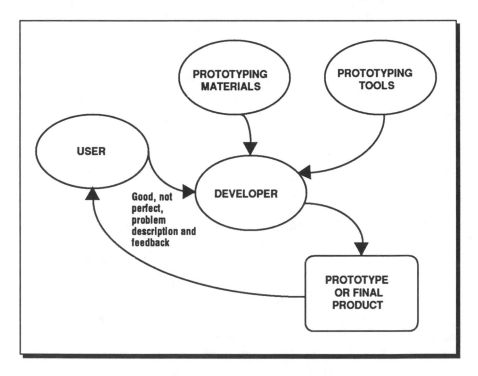

Figure 6-17. A Popular View of Prototyping

What is wrong with this picture? It is missing a way of recording and communicating the design and construction features to others. Without this, the design is limited. Even the designer will not be able to do a good job of reflecting on his or her own work and reviews with others will not be possible because documentation is nonexistent. This limits the usefulness of the application.

But, suppose we add something to the picture as in Figure 6-18.

This revised view makes it an authentic paradigm, because there is now a place to record what took place and to communicate information to the user, to those who will review the program, and to those who will inherit it.

Some Closing Thoughts on the Hardware/ Software Analogy

There is an analogy that software development is like hardware development and that the Waterfall model is equivalent to full-scale production in hardware development. Since the prototype is the precursor of production in hardware, and since the new methods of software development were seen as precursors of the Waterfall process, the word *prototype* was the logical choice.

But, what we mean by prototyping in software is often called a mockup in hardware. The Waterfall process is more like the hardware version of building a prototype. Producing copies of the software, say a PC software application like a word processor, is equivalent to full-scale production.

So, the hardware/software analogy breaks down rather quickly, and the somewhat extended meaning of the word *prototype* loses the force of its antecedents.

A more accurate analogy is in lithography, where a master plate is constructed by an artist and copies are produced by imprinting the design onto paper using ink as the transfer medium. But, this analogy also breaks down quickly. In lithography, the plate is made of one material, the copies of another. The physical media of software, whether it be master or copy, is the same. It is stored as magnetic patterns and used as electronic signals. The media on which both master and copy can reside may be identical. This is important because the prototype can then become the product.

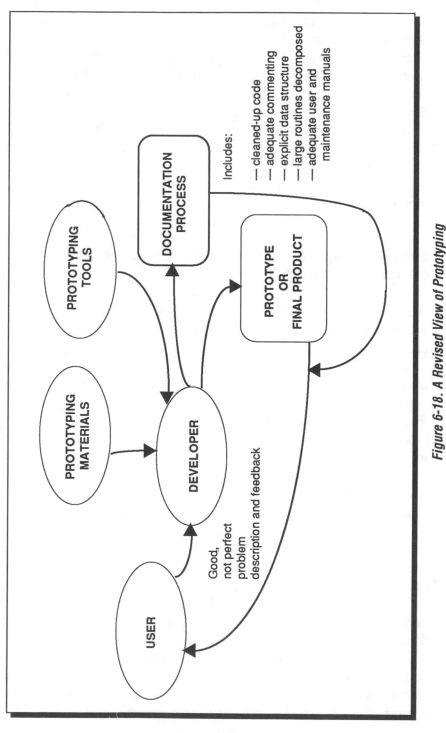

Figure 6-18. A Revised View of Prototyping

Includes:

— cleaned-up code
— adequate commenting
— explicit data structure
— large routines decomposed
— adequate user and
   maintenance manuals

PROTOTYPING TOOLS

PROTOTYPING MATERIALS

DOCUMENTATION PROCESS

PROTOTYPE OR FINAL PRODUCT

DEVELOPER

USER

Good, not perfect problem description and feedback

Reusability

Reusable code is often the proto-system used in prototyping. It is one of the current buzz words in our field, and it is being treated as something new. But, when you really examine it, you find it has been in use for a long time.

One of the earliest reusable things was the computer itself. One day it was an accounting machine, the next day it was a text processor, and the next day it was a CAD/CAM system. The machine and its operating system are reused quite a bit.

Run-time libraries are another example. They might perform special system services, or mathematics, statistics, or graphics functions. In addition, source code is often reused.

Designs such as structure charts and data-flow diagrams (DFDs) can be reused. For example, NASTEC has a way of creating a library of data-flow diagrams that you can call into your own design and edit any way you want. So, if you are working on avionics systems, you can bring general avionics data-flow diagrams into your workspace and modify them the way you want. You do not have to start over from scratch.

You can reuse other materials such as trade studies, market information, and proposal information.

Reusability allows you to pay attention to the unique, creative, "problem solving" aspects of your problem—not the common aspects.

Finally, optimized modularity, coupling, and cohesion are key to reusing source and object code. Kenneth Shere provides a concise discussion of them in *Software Engineering and Management.* [Shere 1988, pp.28-31]

Summary

Prototyping is a less formal method of software development. It starts with some kind of proto-system and incomplete requirements. The developer changes the proto-system to meet the requirements, verifies them and, if more emerge, repeats the process. If not, then he completes the documentation and is finished.

Prototyping is used outside the Waterfall, either before it to limit risk or demonstrate concepts or after it in extended development and maintenance. It is used inside the Waterfall to get better requirements and can be used as a replacement for it.

Many good claims are made for the benefits of prototyping and there is some evidence that they are true. It gives us greater control over the problem and attracts the cooperation of outside users. However, prototyping suffers from a bad reputation, bad documentation, and sometimes produces systems with poor performance.

Toward the end of the Age of Faith, a series of great thinkers and observers redefined the human race's place in the universe. Nicholas Copernicus postulated that the planets revolve around the sun, not the earth. Galileo Galilei discovered that earth was not the only center of rotation when he discovered the moons of Jupiter. Tycho Brahe made careful observations about heavenly bodies, especially Mars; Johannes Kepler used these observations to describe how the planets moved; and Sir Issac Newton used gravity to explain why.

Together, these remarkable men moved humanity away from the center of the universe and, as it turned out, toward the center of knowledge. No longer do we have to depend on the "Revealed Word" for information about everything. Now, we depend on ourselves.

And so it is with prototyping. For too long we have dangled at the ends of enormous computing and organizational systems that intimidate us with their scale. Now, with prototyping, we no longer depend for success on processes "revealed" to us and the great "shoulds" about programming. Prototyping, by showing one alternative, moves us away from that "Revealed Word" to a place where we can depend on ourselves for our knowledge about solving problems with computers. It brings things back to a human scale. It makes the computer a tool and allows us to make the tool fit the hand rather than the other way around.

CHAPTER SEVEN
The All-at-Once Model

The traditional view of software development is to associate a phase with activities of the same name. Thus, the Requirements phase is associated with requirements activities. This traditional view also holds the opposite to be true—that requirements activities are associated with the Requirements phase and that the activities are bound to the phase.

However, this is not quite true. As Zelkowitz observed, all phases include activities commonly thought to be performed in other phases. [Zelkowitz 1988, pp.331, 336]

In prototyping, this begins to unravel a little more. If you did prototyping to gather requirements, then design, coding and testing were part of that step in a big way. This was true even though these activities were to be repeated when the "real" phases associated with them were begun.

In this chapter, we encounter approaches to software development where activities are bound to other *activities*, and not to phases. They are called "all-at-once" because all the "phases" seem to be done concurrently. Actually, they are a class of one-phase approaches. (See Figure 7-1.)

The All-at-Once model is similar to the Prototyping model in that during some time period many activities related to traditional phases are going on concurrently. But, it is different in that an outside observer would not see the activities as separate. To this outside observer, it looks like all the activities are done at the same time. This, at first, seems like the "undisciplined" hacking Boehm rightly complains about. However, it is not that at all. It is the way many people develop software when they not only do not know the solution, but they also do not know the problem—when they are trying to solve wicked problems.

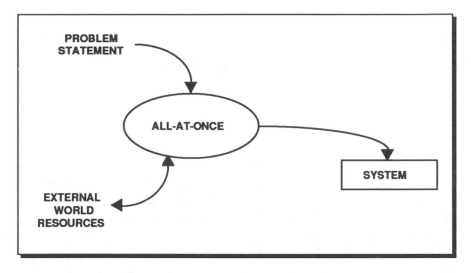

Figure 7-1. The All-at-Once Model

The All-at-Once model occurs in several forms. There are team, two-man, and one-man approaches. They all have many of the same general characteristics, but are they unique in important ways and have different histories.

Team Approaches—Sashimi and Scrum

Let us begin with the team approaches, Sashimi and Scrum. The Sashimi approach originated with the Japanese and their experiences with the Waterfall model. [Takeuchi and Nonaka 1986]

The Japanese adopted the Waterfall model early on and found many of the problems with it that others have. In addition, they saw that speed and flexibility were as important in product development as traditional high quality, low cost, and product differentiation. So, as they have done with so many other things, they adapted it to their own style. They reduced the number of steps to four, but did not remove any activities. This caused, in effect, an overlap among traditional phases. And, they made the four phases themselves overlap. They called it Sashimi, named for the Japanese way of presenting the sliced raw fish dish, where each slice rests partially on the slice before it. (See Figure 7-2.)

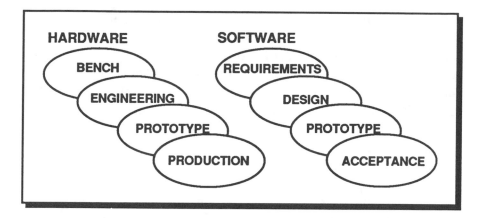

Figure 7-2. The Sashimi Approach

The model that is labeled *hardware* represents the Fuji-Xerox product development schedule. The one labeled *software* is my interpretation of how the four hardware phases would be renamed for a software project.

Other companies went a step further. They reduced the number of steps from four to one and gave it a name from rugby. In rugby, everybody on the team acts together with everybody else to "move the ball down the field." This team pack is called a Scrum. (See Figure 7-3.)

As you can see, the Sashimi approach is like the Waterfall model, except that much of the end of one phase is coincident with the preceeding phase. At first glance, this is not so new. Many people have suggested an overlap as part of the Waterfall model. But, they usually meant the validation procedure which, if it failed, caused the input to be sent back to the previous phase. Practitioners of Sashimi intend that there be close communication and integration between the overlapping phases, and that there be close cooperation between adjoining phases.

If Scrum were applied to software development, it would go something like this:

Suppose you have a software development project to do. For each traditional phase, you can draw from a pool of experienced people. Rather than have several designers do the design phase and have several coders do the construction phase, etc., you form a team by carefully selecting one person from each pool. During a team meeting, you will tell them that they have each been carefully chosen to do a project that is very important to the company, country, organization, or whatever. This unsettles them somewhat. You then give them a description of the problem to be solved, the figures for how much it cost in time and money to do similar projects, and what the performance figures for similar systems are. Then, after you have gotten them used to the idea that they are special, having been specially chosen and challenged to do an important job, you further unsettle the team by saying that their job is to produce the system in, say, half the time and money and it must have twice the performance of other systems. Next, you say that *how* they do it is their business. Your business is to support them in getting resources. Then, you leave them alone.

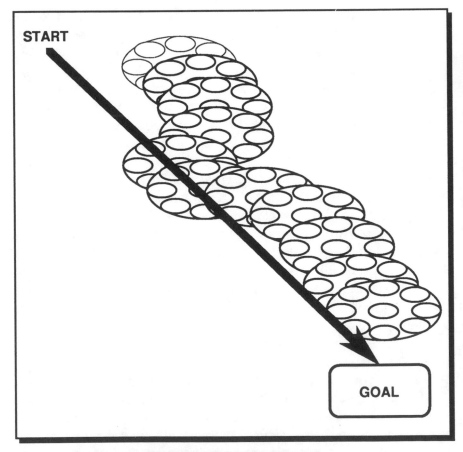

Figure 7-3. The Scrum Approach

You stand by to give them advice if you are asked. You get their reports, which come regularly but not as often nor as voluminously as with the Waterfall model. But, mostly you wait. In something like the appointed time, out pops the system with the performance and cost figures you wanted.

Sounds like a fairy tale doesn't it? But that is precisely how Honda produced the City car, how Canon produced the PC-10 personal copier, the AE-1 single lens reflex camera, and the Sure Shot, and how NEC produced the PC8000 personal computer.

So, how does it work? Well, getting back to our story, after this extraordinary meeting concludes and you leave the room, each member of the team starts to adjust to the idea. Some of the team members might decide they want no part of your hairbrained scheme and check out immediately. But, others will accept the challenge; they will integrate the objective.

After a while magic happens. It is slow at first and hardly noticeable, but soon the team begins to stir. Strange things begin to happen. There was an initial "official" leader, but soon he becomes the designated reporter. Another leader appears during one part of the work, but she is only temporary and soon another leader takes her place. Soon, it is noticed that the system testers are learning more and more about how to do requirements. After a while, they begin to actually contribute to the requirements discussions. The person writing the requirements is also writing them from the testing point of view: "How can we test this?"

A testing specialist might ask during requirements discussions, "Does this lead to simple designs?" She has the sense of the requirements because she not only helped to write them, but has come to trust that all the others have taken into account whatever they have learned from each other about the important elements in the other steps of the system's development.

When testing is discussed, others take an interest and learn and then contribute to *that* discussion. And when they do begin to contribute to the testing plans, she welcomes their participation.

In fact, as the work done in each of the phases is discussed, all the others learn about it and begin to contribute to it. Whenever any member of the team does some work, he is doing it with the full force of all the members.

It is as if anyone doing any work is building the finished product. When someone writes code, they are also writing requirements, functional specifications, and design notes at the same time. The steps are done "all-at-once," and that is where the name derives.

More than likely, the team will toss out its first notion of the system. But, this is to be expected. It is common in any method and even more so here because old things have to be unlearned along with learning new things. But, as they proceed, the final concept, design and finished product emerge from the team's work.

This is not a child's game or a "too cutsy" faddish gimmick for "sharing the experience." This is a serious process by which people get committed to accomplishing something. So committed, in fact, that sometimes they suffer much emotional pain when the project is completed.

The team becomes autonomous and the members start to act like entrepreneurs. (Some use the term "intrapreneurs.") The team tends to transcend their initial goals, going for maximum excellence. The members learn from and teach each other. And, this method works. It has a history of success in Japan.

The Scrum approach works by reducing the need for lengthy, passive, third-person communication, reporting, and authorization ceremonies. And, it substitutes short, active, first- and second-person communication and fewer contacts with "external" entities. Its basic premise is that if you are committed to the team and the project, and if your boss really trusts you, then you can spend time being productive—not justifying your work.

Takeuchi and Nonaka identify the following elements in "moving the scrum downfield":

- Built-in instability
- Self-organizing project teams
- Overlapping development phases
- "Multilearning"
- Subtle control
- Organizational transfer of learning

In our example, the instability was provided by management first when it announced the importance of the project and again when it challenged the team to excel with a significant new product.

Management did not provide much framework for organization and left most of it up to the team, which changed its leaders and other the components of the organization as necessary.

Whether Sashimi or Scrum, all of the efforts were characterized by overlapping phases and there was much more acceptance and exchange of other's views.

It was commonly reported that team members learned each other's jobs. And, their own "native" expertise profited as a result, "widening" their fields of expertise. This also contributed to added *depth* of expertise because of added insight from *wider* experience. For example, design engineers develop better when they have an understanding of how and whether their design can be produced. Team members gain these insights from the process.

To be sure, control *is* exercised; but, it is subtle and much of it is indirect. It is exercised by selecting the right people, creating an open work environment, encouraging feedback from the field, establishing an evaluation and reward system based on group performance, managing the tendency for going off in many directions early on and the need to integrate information and effort later on, tolerating and even anticipating mistakes, and encouraging suppliers to become involved early without controlling them.

Finally, the team members spread the word and their learning was transferred by word of mouth to other projects and the organizations themselves. The organizations institutionalized some of it by creating standards and emulating the scrummed project.

This model fills in the "what/how" gap. As development proceeds, the range of solutions is apparent and continuously narrowed. In addition, the vertical integration of the technique, where each team member develops an understanding of all the steps involved in solving at least part of the problem, makes it possible to bridge the gap inside the human mind. What you have then is the beginning of a really professional point of view. A person takes his understanding of the problem, associates it with a range of solutions he has studied and, using skill, intelligence, and experience, narrows the range to one or a few options.

During the Scrum procedure, partial solutions are frequently being produced. This is useful when you have to produce something new, like a new motorcycle, to beat the competition. When you are trying to produce something new, not only do you not know the solution, but you also do not know the problem. Otherwise, it would not be new—a wicked problem.

As you might imagine, using the Scrum approach would take some courage on the part of management even with the success of the Japanese economy to use as support. The question, then, is can it be transplanted without modification?

It would be difficult, and sometimes even impossible, to give up the control that it takes to support the Scrum method. In the first place, the government, as a customer, would object since they have a historical need to "oversee" the spending of tax dollars. In the second place, most companies have stockholders with a need for dividends. The Scrum approach is risky.

Finally, there is no guarantee that the team will not run up against real (rather than institutional) limits, which could mean failure of the project. Just as important, however, the disappointment of the failure could adversely affect the team members because of the commitment engendered by the method.

This method is most useful for new product development. In the maintenance environments in which we often find ourselves, large team efforts do not seem to apply.

Another problem of this approach involves the size of the system. We know that systems are becoming larger and more complex. Applying Scrum methods and vertical integration have size limitations, since each team member is asked to understand *all* of the problem and *all* of the steps in developing a system to solve it.

Nevertheless, here are the rugby scores from some Japanese and American corporations: In terms of rapid development, Xerox reduced development time from 5 to 3 years; Brother cut their development time from 4 to 2 years; and John Sculley of Apple computer set a company priority of reducing development time from 3.5 years to 1 year. In terms of flexibility, Black and Decker released 50 new power tool products to compete with Japanese product lines; Honda released 30 new motorcycle models to counter the threat of Yamaha; and IBM broke with tradition by using chips and operating systems for the PC from outside the corporation.

Now, does this have anything to do with the U.S. and software development? Well, many of the products described here were associated with software and some of the companies were U.S. More recently, Chrysler Corporation announced it was reorganizing its engineering operations along the lines of Honda "... to focus emphasis on integrated "whole car" development and overall flexibility and efficiency." [See News Release: *Chrysler Motors Restructures Vehicle Engineering Operations,* Sunday, February 5, 1989.] Added to this are the experiences at General Computer [Kidder 1982] and the success of the Apple Macintosh, including its software.

The Two-Man Approach—Handcuffing

The next "all-at-once" approach is used in "extended development" environments. It is called the Handcuff approach, and is the two-man version of Scrum. As in prototyping, the work usually begins with a seed application or with a program in maintenance that is going to be enhanced.

To produce the final product, the end user (who has a good idea of the problem to be solved) works with the programmer (who is knowledgeable in the computing domain). Often, the end user represents a much larger group and, of course, the programmer represents the group delivering the computing technology. Sometimes, this relationship goes under the name of information center, end-user development, or incremental development. But, it has more in common with Scrum than with any of the other descriptions. (See Figure 7-4.)

EXPERT   PROGRAMMER

Figure 7-4. The Handcuff Approach

This is because they work closely together, learn some of each other's job, take an opportunistic approach to development, and are self-organizing. However, the organizational transfer of learning does not seem to apply. This is probably because of the ad hoc nature of Handcuff. Since it is "unofficial," there aren't many opportunities to transfer learning about the application, programming, or the development experience itself. Nevertheless, the intense focus on the job at hand during the Handcuff method is what characterizes Scrum and all the "all-at-once" methods.

This is the method most familiar to me. I know it is a productive way of working. Of course you should ask, "How can you be objective about this?" Well, in fact, I cannot. There is no healthy way to disconnect oneself from one's experience and one's feelings about the experience. The answers to those questions remain for someone else to answer.

But, I will give a data point from one of my correspondents who also works with this method. He and an engineer did a medium FORTRAN project that was eventually about 80,000 lines of code. They produced the finished code at the rate of 100 lines per day for the team or 50 lines per person per day over a period of about seventeen months. Isn't that somewhere between five and ten times the average we hear about all the time?

This method was put in place because of incomplete requirements again and the nagging problem of not knowing the problem, much less the solution.

For my correspondent, the challenge was to work on the 15,000 lines of extant code that was written without "any real design method," whose presentation was "atrocious," and crashed all the time. In addition, the need for organization in the code was obvious, and this can sometimes become a problem to implement. So, my correspondent was left with a backlog of details he was constantly adding to improve the program.

The engineer knew the application domain and the user community. He had the skill to translate the requirments from that community into code. My correspondent added a "design structure" to the growing program. He improved the presentation of the code, made sure all the routines had appropriate exception handling code added, built tools to help in the development, and instituted a never-ending process of improving the quality of the code between "development" periods.

When it was released, the beta test version simply didn't crash. And, it was a success. It was well received by the user community. Also, management got a return on their investment early on. The released version was used to get further requirements for the next version.

In the Handcuff approach, there often are no noticeable phases in the traditional sense. It is not just that the application expert is doing analysis on the next increment of development while the programmer is still coding and testing the previous one, although that does happen. It is more a matter of selecting the work that is most likely to have the best effect from a long list of tasks from all the phases of development. It is opportunistic.

The thing that is most frequently reported by my correspondents about the Handcuff approach is "multilearning." On teams where there is mutual respect, a transfer of knowledge and expertise takes place. In my case, I was able to comment on "engineering" issues after a while, and was even invited to attend a class designed to increase the number of engineers in the field I was supporting. This was done not to upgrade my knowledge, but to determine if I wanted to *become* an engineer in that field. I had learned enough about the field that it would not take much more training before I would actually be qualified to work in the field. Conversely, the engineers with whom I worked frequently learned from me about programming.

Initially, a Handcuffed team is self-organizing. There is an application expert and a programming expert. However, an application expert frequently tries to transfer his or her sense of expertise to programming, requiring the programmer member to become a drudge—a hack in the literary sense of the word. I was luckier; my teammates were eager to learn what I had to offer. There is an ongoing problem, however, with the inappropriate attribution of expertise of what I call a "darkside power user" and what Ledgard calls an amateur. This is someone who knows the application area but does not necessarily have an understanding of the programming issues that we are so laboriously bringing to light. Typically, programs written by these quasi-professionals have long and complex routines with many backward-branching control statements. These programs are characterized by nonexistent data definitions and mysterious data structures. Commenting is usually sparse, as is documentation. And, these programs crash a lot.

In a Handcuff environment, the programmer is often working to improve these attributes. But, I have the impression that the programmer is being humored because the user understands that, in the programmer's field, much work is done before anything of value results. This perception is part of the legacy of the Waterfall model. "Real" programming is done by engineers.

Subtle control is exercised, but it is more like the programmer is on temporary duty in the engineer's organization. And, so, the reporting and documenting become more practical.

There are two important advantages here for management. First, there is an early return on investment because it is never intended that all the requirements be discovered or implemented at once. So, programs that do some useful work are produced, put in place, and used. Meanwhile, the next version is in development. This process is repeated for the period for which management signed up.

Second, management can plan more effectively and simply. Management is asked to allocate the team labor and resources for one year. This coincides with typical budgeting cycles. And, their commitment is limited. After a year in which something useful has probably been done, a decision is made about spending the next increment of resources for the next increment of the program. If the decision is made to not continue, you have what has already been done. But, consider the Waterfall: there is not very much of use produced until late in the project, and a year is a short time with that model.

There are several problems with the Handcuff approach. First, it is not very useful for new development since it needs some sort of a seed. Strangely, I have never seen it operate *without* some sort of seed program; it has no history of new development. This could very well be a reaction to the heavy front-end work required by the Waterfall. Sometimes, Artificial Intelligence applications are developed from "scratch" by an expert and an AI guy working together, but there is usually some software available to help them. If any of you have Handcuff experience that did not include a seed, please let us know by way of the reader response card in the back.

Second, expertise is often unevenly attributed. The user usually has more "standing" than the programmer who is considered merely a "skilled aide." As a result, the application is often "hacked" out, with a low rating in several of the essential characteristics that make up a professionally written program.

In the example I gave at the beginning of the discussion, and in spite of the best efforts of my colleague, he judged that the program could not be maintained. Try as he might, there just was not enough time to decompose the routines that needed it, to add adequate comments, to reveal the essential data structure, or to use the data structure to make the program structure coherent. There were no context diagrams or other navigational aids except the ones he drew in self defense.

Part of this uneven skill attribution is due to a user's perception of the programming side's inability to produce anything in a timely way, and without reams of paperwork, and with *much* too many meetings, and for too much money. (In other words, their perception of the Waterfall model.)

However, the advantages of the Handcuff approach are substantial—high productivity, an early (and usually good) return on investment, which also utilizes available resources more efficiently, simplified planning, and very good risk control.

The One-Man Approach—Hacking

The one-man version of Scrum is Hacking. By hacking, I mean combining an intimate knowledge of the problem to be solved with knowledge and skill in programming. I do not mean hacking in the literary sense of a servile worker writing anything for pay. What is key here is an intimate knowledge of the problem and substantial skill. And, of course, this includes the bad connotation attached to the term. (See Figure 7-5.)

Hackers have a bad reputation. They are blamed for the viruses that currently afflict us. We read about hackers breaking into secure computer systems and networks and finding ways to defeat the telephone company's billing system. There are stories about hackers entering electronic funds transfer streams and making off with some money.

Figure 7-5. Hacking

Most hackers aren't bad folks. They are often people with expertise in one field who discover programming and expect to transfer their expertise without learning the skills needed to do professional programming. Power users are often in this category.

These are also the folks who, to a large extent, gave us our computer revolution today. I am talking about people like Bill Gates (Microsoft), John Warnock (Adobe), Jeff Raskin (Macintosh), Gary Kildall (CP/M), and many others.

To give you the sense of hacking as I understand it, consider the following parable:

The Parable of the Two Programmers[1]
by Neil W. Rickert
Department of Math, Stat., and Computer Science,
University of Illinois at Chicago

Once upon a time, unbeknown to each other, the "Automated Accounting Applications Association" and the "Consolidated Computerized Capital Corporation" decided that they needed the identical program to perform a certain service.

Automated hired a programmer-analyst, Alan, to solve their problems.

Meanwhile Consolidated decided to ask a newly hired entry-level programmer, Charles, to tackle the job, to see if he was as good as he pretended.

Alan, having had experience in difficult programming projects, decided to use the PQR structured design methodology. With this in mind he asked his department manager to assign another three programmers as a programming team. Then the team went to work, churning out preliminary reports and problem analyses.

Back at Consolidated, Charles spent some time thinking about the problem. His fellow employees noticed that Charles often sat with his feet on the desk, drinking coffee. He was occasionally seen at his computer terminal, but his office mate could tell from the rythmic striking of keys that he was actually playing Space Invaders.

By now, the team at Automated was starting to write code. The programmers were spending about half their time writing and compiling code, and the rest of their time in conference, discussing the interfaces between the various modules.

His office mate noticed that Charles had finally given up on Space Invaders. Instead he now divided his time between drinking coffee with his feet on the table, and scribbling on little scraps of paper. His scribbling didn't seem to be Tic Tac Toe, but it didn't exactly make much sense, either.

---

[1]The reader is invited to derive his own moral.

Two months have gone by. The team at Automated finally releases an implementation timetable. In another two months they will have a test version of the program. Then a two month period of testing and enhancing should yield a completed version.

The manager of Charles has by now tired of seeing him goof off. He decides to confront him. But as he walks into Charles's office, he is surprised to see Charles busy entering code at his terminal. He decides to postpone the confrontation, so makes some small talk then leaves. However, he begins to keep a closer watch on Charles, so that when the opportunity presents itself he can confront him. Not looking forward to an unpleasant conversation, he is pleased to notice that Charles seems to be busy most of the time. He has even been seen to delay his lunch, and to stay after work two or three days a week.

At the end of three months, Charles announces that he has completed the project. He submits a 500 line program. The program appears to be clearly written, and when tested it does everything required in the specifications. In fact it even has a few additional convenience features which might significantly improve the useability of the program. The program is put into test, and, except for one quickly corrected oversight, performs well.

The team at Automated has by now completed two of the four major modules required for their program. These modules are now undergoing testing while the other modules are completed.

After another three weeks, Alan announces that the preliminary version is ready one week ahead of schedule. He supplies a list of the deficiencies that he expects to correct. The program is placed under test. The users find a number of bugs and deficiencies, other than those listed. As Alan explains, this is no surprise. After all this is a preliminary version in which bugs were expected.

After about two more months, the team has completed its production version of the program. It consists of about 2,500 lines of code.[2] When tested it seems to satisfy most of the original specifications. It has omitted one or two features, and is very fussy about the format of

---

[2] If this seems unreasonable, ask anyone who regularly teaches computer science courses in which programming projects are required. A five to one ratio between the shortest and longest program is quite typical, and usually the shorter programs are better.

its input data. However the company decides to install the program. They can always train their data-entry staff to enter data in the strict format required. The program is handed over to some maintenance programmers to eventually incorporate the missing features.

Sequel:

At first Charles's supervisor was impressed. But as he read through the source code, he realized that the project was really much simpler than he had originally thought. It now seemed apparent that this was not much of a challenge even for a beginning programmer.

Charles did produce about 5 lines of code per day. This is perhaps a little above average. However, considering the simplicity of the program, it was nothing exceptional. Also his supervisor remembered his two months of goofing off.

At his next salary review Charles was given a raise which was about half the inflation over the period. He was not given a promotion. After about a year he became discouraged and left Consolidated.

At Automated, Alan was complimented for completing his project on schedule. His supervisor looked over the program. With a few minutes of thumbing through he saw that the company standards about structured programming were being observed. He quickly gave up attempting to read the program however; it seemed quite incomprehensible. He realized by now that the project was really much more complex than he had originally assumed, and he congratulated Alan again on his achievement.

The team had produced over 3 lines of code per programmer per day. This was about average, but, considering the complexity of the problem, could be considered to be exceptional. Alan was given a hefty pay raise, and promoted to Systems Analyst as a reward for his achievement. [Rickert 1985]

❖❖❖

The hero of the piece is, of course the hacker. When I show this article to my colleagues, they all respond with a knowing smile. Rickert strikes a familiar chord in all of us.

There are two essential qualities described here. First, what we do is to a large extent invisible and, second, we tend to analyze the entire problem in our heads.

This is not to say that leaving a trail (mainly documentation) is not ultimately important. We must write for people as well as for machines. But it is to say that there is an *internal* phase in development, and it ought to be respected and accepted for what it is.

There are two implications here. First, it is perfectly appropriate for developers to stare out the window (this should be understood by the developer's manager) and, second, that once you have the solution in your mind you must express it in such a way that people can understand it. Your product is the program and, if it is to last, it must be comprehensible to both machines and people. This means structured design, a minimum of backward-branching GOTOs, optimized cohesion and coupling, and all the elements of which a professional needs to be aware.

In addition, you must be aware of all the phases as you work out the solution. One of my teachers once commented that he could not see how programs could be written unless you knew something all the way up and down the line (something about all the phases and about the context of the development).

So, what do the hackers say about having the problem in your head? Let us hear from some of them. [Lammers 1986]

Charles Simonyi

Simonyi has worked at the UC Berkeley Computer Center, the Berkeley Computer Corporation, the ILLIAC 4 Project, Xerox PARC, and, since 1981, Microsoft Corporation. While at Xerox, Charles created the Bravo and Bravo X programs for the Alto personal computer. At Microsoft, Charles organized the Application Software Group, which has produced Multiplan, Microsoft Word, Microsoft Excel, and other popular application products.

"The first step in programming is imagining. Just making it crystal clear in my mind what is going to happen. ... Once I have the structure fairly firm and clear in my mind then I write the code." [ibid, p.15]

Bill Gates

As chief executive officer of Microsoft, William H. (Bill) Gates is considered one of the driving forces behind today's personal computing and office automation industry. Gates started his career in computer software at a young age. Both Gates and Microsoft cofounder, Paul Allen, worked as programming consultants while attending high school in Seattle, Washington. In 1974, Gates, then an undergraduate at Harvard University, worked with Allen to develop a BASIC programming language for the first commercial microcomputer, the MITS Altair. After the successful completion of this project, the two formed Microsoft to develop and market software for the emerging microcomputer marketplace.

"You have to simulate in your mind how the program's going to work ..." [ibid, p.73]

John Page

In 1970, Page joined Hewlett-Packard. He provided technical support for HP for four years in London, Geneva, and other parts of Europe. In 1974, he moved to Cupertino, California, the headquarters of Hewlett-Packard, to manage worldwide technical support for the HP 3000 computer. Later, he moved into research and development in software, where he developed the Image Database Management System. While with Hewlett-Packard, Page studied artificial intelligence at Stanford University and did his postgraduate work in computer science.

In 1980, Page left Hewlett-Packard and teamed up with Fred Gibbons and Janelle Bedke to start Software Publishing Corporation. Page, working out of his garage, developed Software Publishing"s first product, which later became PFS: FILE. The PFS series now includes over six programs on all facets of information management. John Page is vice president of corporate research and development for the Software Publishing Corporation.

"I believe very strongly that one person ... should do the design and high-level structure. You get a consistency and elegance when it springs from one mind." [ibid, p.98]

172 • *Wicked Problems, Righteous Solutions*

Jonathan Sachs

Born in 1947, Jonathan Sachs grew up on the east coast, in New England. He earned his bachelor's degree in mathematics at MIT. Sachs spent a total of fourteen years both studying and working at MIT. His experiences there as a programmer were wide ranging: He worked for the Center for Space Research, the Cognitive Information Processing group, and the Biomedical Engineering Center. Sachs developed the STOIC programming language while he was working for the Biomedical Engineering Center.

In the mid-seventies, Sachs left MIT to work at Data General, where he supervised the development of an operating system. Next, he co-founded Concentric Data Systems, a company that is known for its database products. Jonathan Sachs is credited with writing the phenomenally successful Lotus 1-2-3 spreadsheet program. In 1981, Sachs teamed up with Mitch Kapor to develop and promote Sachs' spreadsheet program, and in April 1982, Lotus Development Corporation was formed, with eight employees. On January 26, 1983, Lotus began shipment of 1-2-3 for the IBM PC. By April 26 of the same year, 1-2-3 topped the Softsel best-seller list for the first time, and it has remained at the top ever since. It was the first program to displace VisiCalc. In 1984, Sachs left Lotus to form his own company.

"... I can do anything that I can make an image of in my head."
[ibid, p.169]

Andy Hertzfeld

Born on April 6, 1953, Andy Hertzfeld grew up in the western suburbs of Philadelphia. Hertzfeld became intrigued with computers in high school, where one of the first programs he wrote was a dating program for a school dance. He went on to study physics, mathematics, and computer science at Brown University, eventually earning his degree in 1975. Hertzfeld later earned his master's degree in computer science at the University of California at Berkeley in 1979. After receiving his graduate degree, Hertzfeld went to Apple Computer, where he worked on the Silentype printer, the Apple III operating system, and other products. In February 1981, he joined the Macintosh development group as the second programmer to work on the project, and became the principal developer of the Macintosh operating system. Recently, Hertzfeld left Apple to work independently. He has since developed a program called Switcher for the Macintosh and a low-cost, high-resolution digitizer called ThunderScan.

"To do the kind of programming I do takes incredible concentration and focus. ... keeping all the different connections in your brain at once ..." [ibid, p.260]

What is going on here is more than just having an idea or even imagining some of the functions of a good application. It is having and keeping the whole process in your head, all at once, as Andy Hertzfeld commented.

And, what do they say about the Waterfall model? Here are some examples:

Wayne Ratliff

From 1969 to 1982, C. Wayne Ratliff worked for the Martin Marietta Corporation in a progression of engineering and managerial positions. He was a member of the NASA Viking Flight Team when the Viking spacecraft landed on Mars in 1976, and wrote the datamanagement system, MFILE, for the Viking lander support software.

In 1978, he began writing the Vulcan program, which he marketed by himself from 1979 to 1980. In late 1980, he entered into a marketing agreement with Ashton-Tate and renamed the Vulcan product dBASE II. In mid-1983, Ashton-Tate purchased the dBASE II technology and copyright from Ratliff and he joined Ashton-Tate as vice president of new technology. Ratliff was the project manager for dBASE III, as well as designer and lead programmer.

"... One of the problems this company's struggling with is finding the best way to do software.

"For whatever reason, they don't feel they can trust individuals, or at least a small number of individuals. The procedure now is that Marketing figures out what the program is supposed to do; then Marketing tells Development what they think that is; then

Development spends several months and writes down a very detailed spec of what they think they heard; then many people in the company review that spec and negotiate exactly what it's supposed to do. Then the hard work's over. From then on, it's just coded.

"This process may be appropriate if you're building bridges, because you know exactly what the bridge is supposed to do. It's supposed to go from one side of the river to the other, and you can specify exactly how much maximum weight it's going to carry, and all the other details ahead of time. In fact, with a bridge, I would imagine you can specify everything on one sheet of paper. That's about as much spec as I think a computer program should go through, too: one sheet of paper.

"There's a general agreement in the company that the current process doesn't work, or it's so painful that it's not worth it. It's better to find somebody who has an idea, slip them money under the door, let them work for a long time unhindered, and when they think they're finished with it, you let other people work with the program and make their suggestions about how to improve it." [ibid, p.125]

Peter Roizen

A native Californian, Peter Roizen was raised in Palo Alto. He attended the University of California at Berkeley, where he earned his bachelor's degree in mathematics in 1967. His first job after graduation was as a programmer, although he had very little exposure to programming before that time. Roizen left Berkeley to spend two years in Montreal and Toronto, and then went to Europe, where he worked with the World Health Organization for seven years as a programmer. He later returned to the United States to work for the World Bank in Washington, D.C. In 1980, Roizen started his own company to market and sell the spreadsheet program, T/Maker, which he had worked on in his spare time while employed at the World Bank. In 1985, Roizen moved his small company from Washington D.C. to the San Francisco Bay area.

"In the organization I worked in, many times we never even worked on the problem because we first did feasibility studies that often took longer to do than the piece of work would have taken." [ibid, p.197]

Jonathan Sachs has this to say: "... the standard method for developing a big program, where you spend a lot of time and work up a functional spec, do a modular decomposition, give each piece to a bunch of people, and integrate the pieces when they're all done. The problem with that method is that you don't get a working program until the very end. ..." [ibid, p.167]

Here is what they say about the All-at-Once method:

Gary Kildall: "... Once I get the algorithms down, I start writing code directly on the machine. I don't even write it on a piece of paper before it goes into the computer; it just doesn't seem necessary. ... The magical part is that, at some point, *all at once* the whole thing comes together. ... When I reach the point where the code coalesces, I'm certain the program will work, and I also have no doubt I did it about the best way it could be done. I don't completely understand the process, but it sure seems to work for me, even when I make fairly massive changes to data structures and algorithms." [ibid, p.61. Emphasis added.]

Bill Gates: "The hardest part is deciding what the algorithms are, and then simplifying them as much as you can. It's difficult to get things down to their simplest forms. You have to simulate in your mind how the program's going to work, and you have to have a complete grasp of how the various pieces of the program work together. The finest pieces of software are those where one individual has a complete sense of exactly how the program works. To have that, you have to really love the program and concentrate on keeping it simple, to an incredible degree." [ibid, p.73]

Peter Roizen says: "In the old days, lots of companies made a separation between the analyst and the programmer. The analyst made the overall plan using flowcharts, and the programmer filled in the details. Any time you approach the solution of a problem with some people just drawing boxes and others specifying the contents of the boxes, you inevitably end up with a piece of trash that doesn't solve the problem. When I was a programmer, half the plans I got from analysts were totally unworkable. They have the big picture, but they don't have enough detailed information to do their jobs well. Nobody is clever enough to look at the entire picture and also see details of how the program needs to operate. So I'm for having one person write the program from beginning to end." [ibid, pp.194-195]

So you see, many of the people who are fueling our revolution have long since abandoned the Waterfall model to adapt something else— the All-at-Once method—where they have it all in their heads and clearly visualize it before starting construction. These knights of our age, these software samurai, without being conscious of it are providing the answers about how programmers work and how problems are solved.

The overall theme of this is to have the program in your head. But, if the context of programming, the languages, platforms, organizations, etc., are not given and are not completely understood, the process of visualizing the program is hampered.

Summary

At the far end of the programming spectrum is the All-at-Once model. It has three versions: Scrum/Sashimi, Handcuff, and Hacking. These approaches allow the speed and flexibility required for competing, and provide a context within which programmers can work their magic of visualizing programs in their heads.

There are several more models to look at but, up to this point, this has been the main continuum of how we organize our work. The methods have ranged from orthodoxy to heresy, from outside to inside views, and from distant to intimate relationships to problems.

Finally, the models range from the much talked about Waterfall to the little known All-at-Once. Perhaps now it is time to talk more about the latter and less about the former.

CHAPTER EIGHT
Other Models

In this chapter, I will discuss four other models. Each one has something important to contribute. The first model, Video, is actually composed of three models. They describe unique ways of gathering the data needed for software development and maintenance. The second model, Cleanroom, is an attempt to produce reliable software by preventing errors from entering the process. The third, User Computing, involves programming without programmers, and the fourth model describes system engineering.

Video Models

One of the reasons why prototyping is not well thought of is the "ad hoc" nature of development in a prototyping environment. One of the reasons why Structured Systems Analysis (SSA) in a traditional, top-down, structured analysis and design environment has been hard to implement is the difficult, time-consuming, and error prone methods of collecting data. One reason why maintenance efforts are so difficult is the lack of adequate documentation. The Video model attempts to solve all three problems.

Three writers have something to say about these problems, and they all propose using theatrical methods for solving them.

The Hollywood Model

The first is the Hollywood model proposed by G. R. Gladden in an article entitled "Stop the Life Cycle, I Want to Get Off." [1982] In the article, he discusses the main failings of software development: The software is often late, it is usually incomplete, and it is very prone to errors. He offers the Hollywood model as a solution to these problems.

His solution is based on three propositions:

1. High-level (system) objectives are more stable.

2. A picture is worth a thousand words.

3. High-level system objectives plus physical demonstrations will result in a successful project.

Figure 8-1 is a diagram of his procedure.

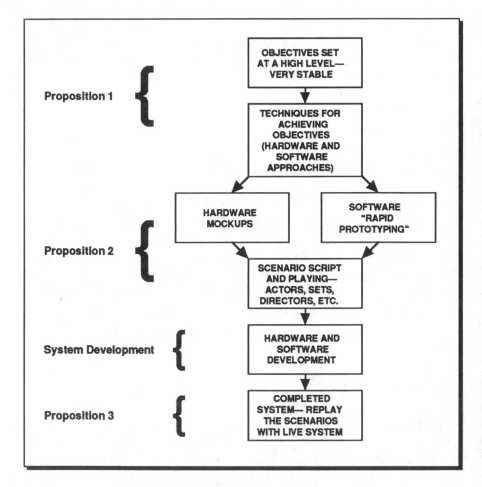

Figure 8-1. The Hollywood Model

His rationale for the first proposition is that high-level system objectives, plus the techniques for achieving them, are less likely to change than requirements are in the traditional Waterfall since they represent longer term, more stable views. And, if the objectives *do* change, the project is likely to go away and not just change.

Earlier, I talked about driving down high-level objectives through a series of language transitions until the final code is produced. (See Figure 8-2.) Gladden steps off that train early, around the initiation step. He wants to take advantage of the relative ease of satisfying high-level objectives. Satisfying objectives is easier than satisfying a lot of the requirements that may have grown out of the objectives, because his proposition allows the details to be dealt with at a lower, more appropriate, level. With the Waterfall model, for example, details grow very rapidly and, by the time the requirements are finished and handed off to developers, they become overwhelming and a source for error.

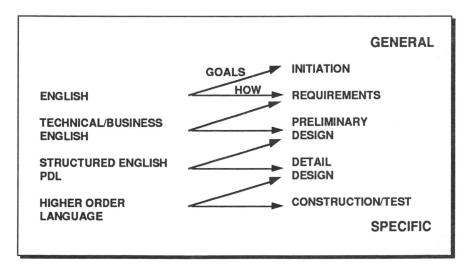

Figure 8-2. Language Transitions

The next proposition is supported by the prototyping activity, which is Gladden's main contribution. He sees software development as "theater," where various actors are playing out roles. The Hollywood model stresses early and active user participation by having demonstrations (mockups) and simulations (prototypes) that the user can exercise. By exercising the mockups and prototypes, the users can help create scripts about how the system is used. They tell the story about how they are using the software and how they do their jobs. These scripts can be acted out by actors as users or by the users themselves and then filmed to record the event for later review by other users and developers.

This method involves the same type of technical people usually used in making movies such as commercial artists, script-writers, film makers, and model makers. These days, the video camera is the most likely tool.

This participation is extremely valuable. First, it helps users (who need intermediate results) to more thoroughly identify and communicate their needs. Second, it produces more accurate data, since it saves scenes that can be replayed later to check and correct observations.

Third, it helps in the validation process. With the Hollywood model, the users have been validating their system bit by bit from the earliest stages and are, therefore, more familiar with it by the time validation takes place. Also, the users and developers know each other better than they would with the traditional Waterfall. With the traditional Waterfall, user committees and developer committees meet to compare notes. With this model, they have a one-on-one familiarity with each other and with each others' ways of doing their jobs. Therefore, they trust each other more easily. There is no need for a long and expensive process to 'validate' the software or a religious-like ceremony to accept it.

Gladden does not say whether his own organization uses his model or what success they have had with it. But, his model shows a lot of promise and seems to be adaptable to many forms of prototyping. The video records that his model produce could provide the formality that many complain is missing in prototyping.

The Outside-In Model

Essentially, the Hollywood model is related to a prototyping development method. But, there is another idea from Henken [1988] that supports the traditional top-down, Structured Analysis and Design method.

Henken first describes the main problem with the traditional, manual way of doing Yourdon-DeMarco Structured System Analysis. He pegs this problem as documenting the current physical model. Yourdon also says that few, if any, actually do this documentation anymore. For Henken, the methods of actually documenting the current physical model are laborious and very time consuming.

One problem in the documentation process is that users usually do not see their system top-down and have a more primitive view, while analysts *start* with the top-down view. Another problem is that the analysts must do two things: interview the user correctly and take accurate notes. They use these notes to produce the elements of the model. But, the interviews are difficult because of the differences in context (top-down for the analyst and primitive for the user), and the notes must be processed and reviewed by the user. By this time, the user is beginning to feel put upon by the process. Henken says that there is a "grave danger [in] SSA that the manual techniques become an end in themselves, maximizing the volumes of documentation rather than optimizing useful information."

But, Henken also needed to reorganize the investigation of systems along lines amenable to video taping, so he introduced a new partitioning as a result, called the inside-out partition. This is where the model gets its name. It is remarkably similar to Jackson System Development and, therefore, the Video Method may also have wide application in that arena.

Henken suggests a partition in which he describes the essential processes of each of the boxes in an organization chart. He uses a context diagram, several outside-in data-flow diagrams, and an analysis diagram that integrates the outside-in DFDs and balances them with the context diagram.

Here is where video comes in. The DFD itself becomes a storyboard and the processes within it become the scenes. The inputs and outputs of each process become the script for each scene. Then each scene, in which users show how outputs are derived from inputs, is taped. These tapes, together with the rest of the outside-in documentation (context diagrams, outside-in DFDs, and analysis DFDs), become the basis for creating the Current Physical Model. In terms of traditional SSA, the mini-specs are recorded on video tape.

This is the way the current physical model is documented. If it is combined with the Hollywood model's theater, the current logical and new physical and logical systems could also be modeled. Developers could then proceed as in the Waterfall model, or they can proceed with the prototype if it becomes usable.

The Maintenance by Television (MTV) Model

The maintenance problem is attacked by Cioch. [1988] Walkthroughs of the system, given by a program expert and, one would suppose, other relevant development activities, are taped and become part of the documentation, which maintenance analysts can use after the developers have left for other projects. Cioch says that this helps programmers ramp up to speed more quickly and comfortably, and this results in greater programmer satisfaction.

Another benefit would be the realization by maintenance programmers that their needs are being met by a state-of-the-art process. This might result in the prestige of maintenance programming being raised somewhat, since most software research money is spent on the front-end work (such as original development and the initial phases of the Waterfall) and maintenance programmers tend to get what is left over.

Video recording retains the context of the event, whether it is a person using a terminal creating information, reading a batch file, or other work. This context is often lost or distorted in documentation. Video records help to fill in the spaces between the paragraphs of more formal written documentation by retaining off-hand remarks, body language, facial expressions (like raised eyebrows), indications of stress in using the program, the ease of using the keyboard, and so on. Since it retains more information than language, which is simply an abstraction of the information on the tape, it retains the information more faithfully.

Video is not new in our field. Many new software products are now being delivered with some sort of audio/visual media, in addition to the normal user's manual. Audio tapes, synchronized to a demonstration of the software, are common. (For example, MacDraw II, for the Macintosh.)

Often, software products are marketed with video-tape demonstration aids. Customers can view these tapes whenever they are ready for the demonstration. One example is the Adobe Illustrator™ software for the Macintosh, which has the software disks, user's manual, and a video overview packaged together. Microsoft Word® also has available a video-tape tutorial, which can be purchased separately. Many CASE tools have demonstration videos available for prospective buyers.

Finally, CD-ROM (compact disk, read-only memory) technology provides a source of audio/video media through the computer itself.

But, using video in the process of developing software is new. This technology can put into the hands of developers and maintainers specific information about the development that often goes undocumented or is embedded in a mass of paper that is obscured by legalese. This technology provides them with a new and powerful user communication tool.

The Cleanroom Model

The Cleanroom model derives its name from its goal: to prevent errors from entering the software development process, just as dirt and debris are excluded from sensitive hardware manufacturing by specially designed production areas equipped with special ventilation and debris-removal facilities. [Dyer and Mills 1981]

The process is illustrated in Figure 8-3. It starts with a complete set of requirements and uses incremental development, stepwise refinement, and independent testing. Its advocates claim that using it reduces the errors in delivered software.

In a study done in 1987 [Selby, Basili, and Baker 1987], there was some confirmation of the claim that this process produced better software. It seemed to produce more complete, less complex software in a timely manner.

The Cleanroom model has three powerful ideas going for it: quality as an integral part of each and every step in development, extensive use of design reviews and code walkthroughs, and statistically-based independent testing.

Quality in every step along the way is a laudable goal. And, I think it is reasonable. It would mean, however, that there be regular measurements made because if the measure is separated for long, the quality loses its meaning. For the Cleanroom model, quality is synonymous with correctness, and both are measures of the match between the implemented solution and the intended requirements.

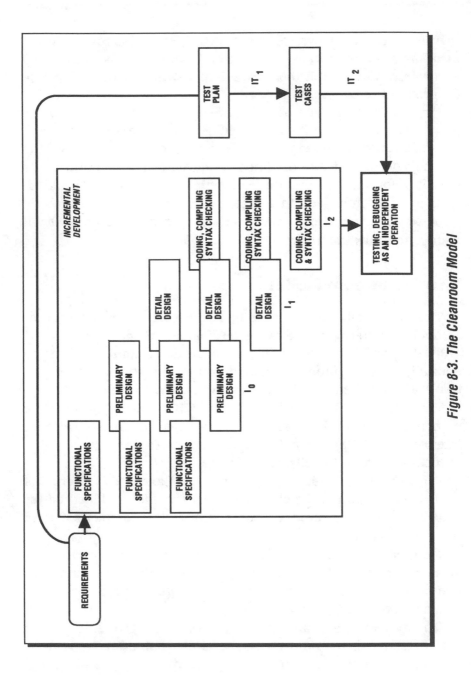

Figure 8-3. The Cleanroom Model

184

There are criteria for each step along the way. For example, in coding one might ask questions like, "Are all the keyword values checked?" "Are all values stored?" or "Are all inputs checked for type and range?"

This correctness is monitored by inspecting the development after preliminary design, detailed design, and coding, called I_0, I_1, I_2. In addition, there are inspections of the test plan and the test cases before testing begins (IT_1, IT_2). And, there are three inspections of the documentation (PI_0, PI_1, PI_2, which are not shown in the figure) at roughly the same points in the publication process.

These inspections are repeated as often as necessary for each cycle of the incremental development method.

I need to make a digression here that is necessary to this discussion. "Inspection" is a daunting word, especially as a part of imposing a new discipline. But, what really goes on during inspection (and this is part of *this* writer's sense of goodness) is a *review* conducted by the designer, coder, or tester with a disinterested party—the moderator.

Reviews are a necessary and usual part of engineering. Reviews do a lot of things, but *all* reviews deal with objectively assessing a piece of work to see if it will do the job. As I indicated earlier, engineers are expected to conduct or participate in reviews. It is part of their job.

In our field, reviews are not nearly as common. One reason is the lack of objectivity one sees in our work and the way developers intimately identify with their work. In these cases, reviews involve inspecting the person as well as the software, and that is always uncomfortable. Sometimes, design reviews exclude "outsiders" as a way of limiting the developer's exposure to criticism.

One of my correspondents reports that project reviews in her organization are conducted discreetly by a team that interviews project members one at a time. Confidentiality is promised, and the results are given to only a few. If the project is politically sensitive, then it is even more discreet.

We aren't yet able to be objective about our work. But, one of the characteristics of professionalism is being able to separate the work from yourself. When we can do that, then we are not dealing with moral issues but technical ones, and then we can learn.

This writer is about to see for himself what review is all about. This manuscript will be run through half-a-dozen editors and some number of reviewers before it finally hits the streets. By the time you read this, the manuscript will have survived the process. But, as I write this, I have some concern about whether *I* will survive.

For example, Figure 8-4 shows "before and after" examples of some paragraphs from this manuscript. In the "before" example, the text appears *exactly* as I originally wrote it. The comments surrounded by asterisks are my partner's demands for amplification of something. The "after" example shows the same material after she rewrote it.

Example One—Before	Example Two—After
One Waterfall I analyzed was composed of 114 major tasks, 87 different organizations, 39 deliverables, and 164 authorizations, for a total of over 400 important items to spend time on.	One Waterfall model I analyzed was composed of 114 major tasks, across 87 different organizations, with 39 deliverables, and 164 authorizations, for a total of over 400 important items on which to spend time.
Most of the deliverable documents act as wampum (***P. how so?***) throughout the life of the project and allows people to talk about it but not do it. The authorizations become ceremonies where guilt is transferred from one organization to another.	Most of these deliverable documents act as "wampum" throughout the life of the project in that people think they have intrinsic value, when in fact they do not. As wampum, these documents allow people to talk about the project, but not actually do the project. In reality, the deliverable documents only have value if the system is completed, just as wampum only has value if someone is willing to take it in trade. But, the plan for the project is treated as if it has as much value as doing the project, with people often staking their reputations and careers on the plan. The authorizations become mere ceremonies in which the guilt is transferred from one organization to another.
One of my correspondents listed four major projects he had worked on. Every one of them were years in length and at least one year longer than estimated when the Design Reviews were conducted which are themselves a long way into the project.	One of my correspondents listed four major projects on which he had worked. Every one of them was years in length, and at least one year longer than estimated when the design reviews were conducted, which were themselves already a long way into the project.

Figure 8-4. An Example of the Editing Process

The effect of the timeliness of production is seen when the project encounters the business decision 'horizon' (***P. Let's talk about what exactly what you mean by the business decision horizon.***) For most businesses there is an expectation that some activity engaged in to increase capacity or productivity takes from two to three years. A new plant can usually be constructed in about this period. However much planning and money are spent before the construction begins, site purchase, permits, architectural plans, etc.	The effect of the timeliness of production is seen when the project encounters the business-decision "horizon." For most businesses, there is an expectation that any activity that is engaged in to increase capacity or productivity should take from two to three years. A new plant, for example, can usually be constructed in about this period of time. This is the business-decision horizon: the length of time to which the business feels it can commit itself for the planned activity. However, much planning and money are spent on the purchase of the site, obtaining permits, developing architectural plans, etc., before the actual construction begins. These activities are not included in the actual construction.
In our business these preliminary activities are included as part of the actual job.	In our business, analogous preliminary activities are included as part of the actual project. As a result, the Waterfall includes a lot more than it should.

Figure 8-4. An Example of the Editing Process (continued)

I have noticed that both producing this manuscript and writing programs involve the same types of experience. First, there is the inside, creative part where imagination is set free. This is very personal, and I *do* identify with it. Then, there is the outside, public part where the products of imagination can be judged objectively (or so I hope) by reviewers or users. The transition between the two is mysterious, and I don't quite understand it. However, when the public review process takes place, we have a chance to improve the quality of the internal, creative part. Because, as I indicated earlier in this digression, *all* reviews deal with objectively assessing a piece of work to see if it will do the job.

Now, we'll return to the Cleanroom. With the Cleanroom model, testing is done independently of the developers. Testers have a test plan and test cases that were developed and checked earlier in parallel with the design and code activities. These test cases were chosen based on the frequent distribution of system inputs and different system states. They run the test cases, keep track of failures, compute a measure of the system reliability, and report back on the results. This process has many of the merits and few of the liabilities of user-detected errors.

Testers see the program as an input to their process. They have not built up as many distortions and blind spots as the developers may have in the process of transforming ideas to programs, private to public, inside to outside.

All three of the major notions of the Cleanroom model—quality being introduced all the way through the process, inspections before the program is executable (but while the programmers are), and independent testing—make up a powerful *troika* of techniques that are lacking in much of our work.

As I reported earlier, empirical results of software development show that walkthroughs are a predictor of reliable programs. In addition, some early success for the Cleanroom model was due to the savings inherent in incremental development because it is a way to control costs and provide an early return on investment (ROI).

However, there are some problems with this model. First, in the study often cited, there was no check on the main claim about errors being reduced. The investigators looked at operational completeness, successful test cases, and measures of quality and performance, but error rates were missing from the study. And, they seemed to think that the "chief programmer" method works well. However, that is not verified in the investigation that I cited earlier. [Card, et. al 1987]

Second, the model starts with the requirements already finished. It hardly seems like a fair trial of a development method to hold constant something that everyone knows is not constant.

The third problem is the "true believer" atmosphere of those who advocate it. Here are some words used by advocates about what they would do to programmers: "*impose discipline* on software developers," "*enforcing a new discipline* on system developers," "individuals can be *taught to write correct* programs," "designers will most probably be more *conscientious* in their code development." [Emphasis added.]

One gets the impression of a stern abbot in a monastery, imposing a fasting discipline on monks sitting in their cubicles copying out bibles and other books, or worse. Of course, "goodness" is desirable and "badness" is not. But, the true believer's attitude starts with the "badness" of programmers, and that is not professional.

The Cleanroom model is a step in the right direction. However, we ought to be concerned about the military nature of that step. This military nature will stifle creativity.

User Computing

By user computing, I mean former users being able to do without programmers to get their work done by using powerful tools such as code generators, fourth-generation languages (4GLs), application generators, and a host of software such as Lotus, Excel, R:Base, and Hypercard on personal computers. The applications developed by these programs used to be developed by programmers using third-generation languages (3GLs) and are now being developed by users using 4GLs.

Most 4GLs, such as Focus and Ramis II, are for business systems: but one, Gibbs, is for scientific work. Focus is from Information Builders Inc., Ramis II is from Mathematica Inc., and Gibbs is being developed at Cornell University. [Cornell Theory Center 1984]

There are two "flavors" of 4GLs. One type is the code generator. (See Figure 8-5.)

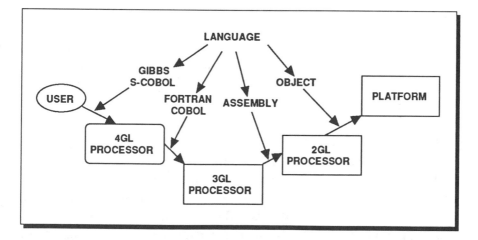

Figure 8-5. A Code-Generator 4GL

Here, the 4GL S-COBOL transforms the easier-to-write code into a 3GL COBOL code, which the programmer is trying to avoid using directly. The 3GL transforms its input into 2GL Assembly. That processor performs yet another transformation into machine code, which the computer executes.

The other flavor is the application generator. Usually, the situation is like that in Figure 8-6.

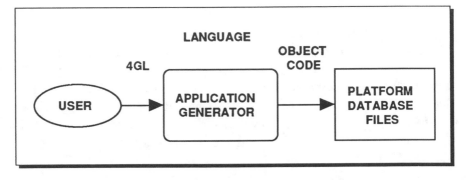

Figure 8-6. An Application-Generator 3GL

Here, the developer uses a 4GL to interact with the application generator, which prepares a database query, which is processed by the database, which sends the results back to the user. There are no intermediate versions of the code. Back in Chapter Six, this was the preferred tool for prototyping.

In both cases, the 4GL used is usually nonprocedural. Unlike procedural languages, which require the programmer to specify inputs, outputs, and *how* to transform the input to the output, nonprocedural languages require that the programmer specify only the input and output. The 4GL processor supplies the transformation. This means that the generator contains a number of transforming functions. And, that means the number of applications that can be written in 4GLs are fewer than with 3GLs.

Each generation of computer language reduces the amount of code that has to be written by roughly an order of magnitude. If the second-generation language, usually called the assembler, required 1,000 lines of code to accomplish some task, then the 3GL would require 100 lines, and the 4GL would require 10 lines. And, one would expect a potential productivity gain of roughly 10:1 over the 3GL. However, in practice it is usually somewhat less, especially at the introduction of the language. But in the case of 4GLs, there are claims of productivity gains higher than 10:1. [Burroughs Corp.]

It is as if the 4GL and its processors took the place of the programmer in the Handcuff paradigm. The knowledgeable user and his problem remain, but communication with the computer expert goes away.

A variation on this theme is an information center, where users still produce the software, but are coached in the use of the tools by experts. These are not always programmers. Sometimes users become expert in using some application or another and provide the expertise to other users. But, the key thing is that there does not need to be an intermediary between the user and the computer. The user becomes a hacker, and I mean that in both senses of the word. Since he has a powerful tool available, he can imagine solutions to his problems and work them out with the tool. Since he most likely has no training in the collected wisdom of programming, he will most likely produce what might charitably be called "unstructured" code. But, if he writes software that gets the job done and if the tool keeps him from producing error-prone code, *so what.* And, if "real" programmers tend to shy away from 4GLs, others who use them report that they are versatile, flexible tools that actually help people work.

Many people have been skeptical about the 4GLs. Some claim 4GLs aren't "real" languages. Others are skeptical about the productivity claims.

Well, it is true that they are limited and still require some procedural code to be supplied in order to be extended to a wider range of applications. One correspondent confirmed that a 4GL she was using produced only a subset of the applications needed in her shop. Those that needed complex processing were still done in COBOL. But, the jobs the 4GLs can do are well received and, as experience with them grows and they are improved, they will find applications in more and more of the application backlog. And, limits are not necessarily a bad thing.

There is a story about Michelangelo encountering a block of marble that had a flaw. This flaw limited its possibilities. It had been rejected by many other sculptors because they were not able to use it for their work. But the master saw something in it and produced his David. The other sculptors have gone away, but Michelangelo and his David remain.

There is some evidence that the productivity claims for 4GLs are true. In a famous study [*A Programmer's Productivity Controversy*, EDP Analyzer; and Martin 1985, p.84], also reported by E.E. Rudolph [Burroughs Corporation] using the function point metric to measure the productivity of Burroughs' 4GL, Linc, he found that it took 14 lines of Linc to create a function point opposed to 114 for COBOL and 62 lines of PL/1. In addition, it took one hour per function point opposed to from 20 to 50 hours (depending on the size of the program) for COBOL. And, since the programmer replaces the 4GL in the Hacking and Handcuff models, I believe that Rudolph's study provides indirect evidence for the claims of higher productivity for those two paradigms as well.

Slowly, the computer is being brought to all of us to use. And, as all of us find a use for it, some of us will have to change jobs.

System Engineering

Daniel Appleton describes a very large project. [Appleton 1986] A company started out by wanting to replace its cost and scheduling systems. A first glance showed that they needed to be replaced, and it looked like a 5-megabuck deal.

The new system was further subdivided into 13 major functions and the cost went to 10 megabucks. Teams were created to evaluate 11 of the 13 functions. Each team was composed of 5 people who were mainly users. The teams decomposed the functions into 700 requirements and gave a new cost estimate of 20 megabucks.

Constraints were now added: no more than 50 developers and 20 megabucks! By the time the disaster happened, there had been 4 different project managers, and 2 different user team leaders. "It began to dawn on people that this was no longer a project, or even a system. No one was sure what it was." [ibid]

He goes on: "Once again the original project was not a project at all. It was a dream. This dream, when stuffed into the big end of a structured, functional decomposition system development methodology, not only got stuck, it turned into a nightmare. Managers then had to face the problem of how to divide the nightmare into some doable projects, each of which had the potential of becoming a nightmare itself. The only known algorithm known to successfully decompose very large projects into doable projects was practiced in secret by the Druids. Most IS managers depend on miracles." [ibid]

He offers help in two ways.

First, assess the project based on 11 criteria. Then, rate the project on a scale of 1-10 for each criteria. Add up the total score and, if it is higher than 90, the project is do-able. If it is lower, then "you have an incipient very large project on your hands." Here are the criteria:

1. Does the proposed project automate a known static process?

2. How "tight" is its scope: how many interfaces are there with existing systems?

3. Does it replace more than one existing system?

4. How few and fixed are the requirements?

5. How complex are the requirements?

6. Is the estimated total development no more than 12 months?

7. Is there a dedicated development environment?

8. Is there an established software, database architecture?

9. Does a single individual have responsibility and authority for project success?

10. Is a formal system development methodology strictly enforced?

11. Are knowledgeable users committed to the project?

Second, he offers the asset-based life cycle shown in Figure 8-7.

This model is a way to create and manage assets that can be reused to do other work. It starts with a requirements evaluation. Then, a decision is made on how to create and assemble them into the system to be shipped: use assets directly from the asset inventory, customize assets that are already there, or make some from

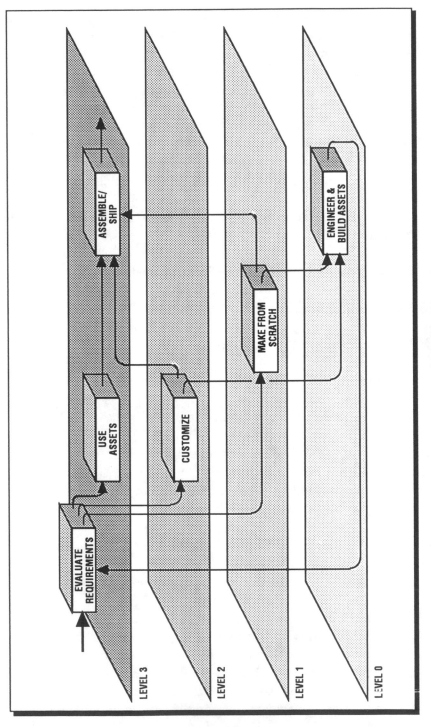

Figure 8-7. An Asset-Management Model

LEVEL 3

LEVEL 2

LEVEL 1

LEVEL 0

194

scratch. If you customize an asset or make one from scratch, the developers go through a process of converting it into a new asset. Appleton does not specify what would go on, but it is reasonable that the new asset needs to be cataloged, and perhaps made portable, robust, and able to be modified. Then, it is entered into the inventory.

In addition, Appleton describes the environment in which this management takes place. It has three parts: an information architecture that deals with requirements, a computer systems architecture that manages the hardware and operating system software, and a control architecture that contains planning, system development, and project-management procedures, as well as technical and data standards and quality assurance.

What he describes is a systems engineering organization where project evaluation ratings and asset management would be done routinely as a part of the initial planning. Appleton's model does not show a make or buy process, and that is certainly a part of the deliberations. But, his three-part architecture is right on. I have noticed time and again that when systems engineering is missing from projects, they are difficult to contain and they evolve into the monsters managers have nightmares about. One correspondent, who reviews projects a lot, agreed and has often asked me when this book will be out.

Another view of System Engineering comes from the *System Engineering Management Guide,* produced by Defense Systems Management College, Fort Belvoir, Virginia. It presents the Department of Defense's (DoD) view of the subject.

"System Engineering is most active in the planning period and in conceiving the system concept and defining the requirements for the system. As the detailed design is being finalized, system engineers resolve the interface problems, do tradeoff analyses, and assist in verifying performance. During the production phase, System Engineering is primarily concerned with verifying system capability and maintaining the baseline system. During the operations period [it] evaluates changes to the system, establishes their effectiveness and facilitates the effective incorporation of changes, modifications and updates." [Defense Systems Management College 1983, p.1-1]

Figure 8-8 shows the main elements of System Engineering from the DoD's point of view, followed by the composition of each element.

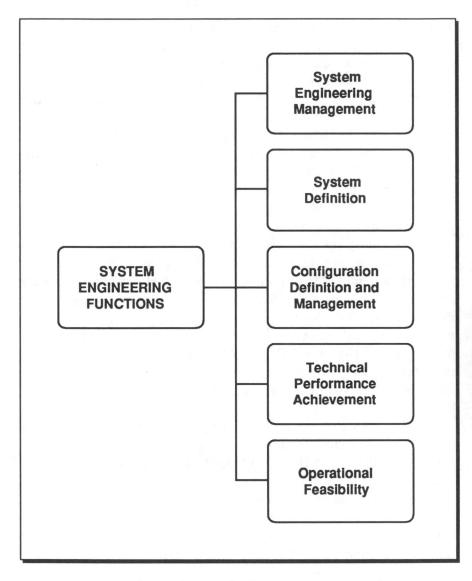

Figure 8-8. System Engineering From the DoD's Point of View

System Engineering Management is concerned with:

1. Organization
2. System Hierarchy
3. System Integration
4. Work Breakdown Structures

System Definition looks at:

1. System Definition and Mission Requirements Analysis
2. Functional Analysis
3. Requirements Flowdown and Allocation
4. Trade Studies
5. System Synthesis

Configuration Definition and Management is charged with:

1. Specification Generation
2. Configuration Management

Technical Performance Achievement looks at:

1. Risk Analysis and Management
2. Technical Performance Measurement
3. Performance Verification

Operational Feasibility is concerned with:

1. Engineering Specialty Integration
2. System Effectiveness
3. Life Cycle Cost and Design To Cost
4. Logistics and the Logistics Support Analysis Process
5. Modification Management
6. Manufacturing and Producibility

Also in the manual is a chart showing the typical Contractor System Engineering organization. The chart is shown in Figure 8-9 together with a breakdown of each component. I have modified it somewhat to make it applicable to general technical and business organizations.

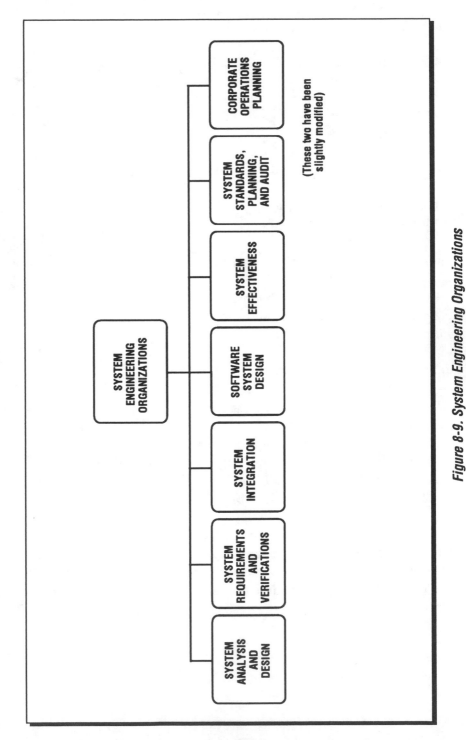

Figure 8-9. System Engineering Organizations

The SYSTEM ANALYSIS AND DESIGN organization provides:

1. Mission Analysis
2. System Trades Studies
3. System Configuration
4. System Performance
5. Technical Performance Measurement
6. Risk Analysis
7. Cost Analysis

The SYSTEM REQUIREMENTS AND VERIFICATIONS organization performs:

1. System Specifications
2. Requirements Flowdown and Traceability
3. Design Reviews
4. Performance Verification
5. Configuration Control Board Activities
6. Risk Management

The SYSTEM INTEGRATION organization:

1. Analyzes Interfaces
2. Defines Interface Requirements
3. Ensures Interface Compatibility
4. Prepares System Integration Plans and Documents
5. Supports an Interface Control Group
6. Issues and Tracks Revision Notices

The SOFTWARE SYSTEM DESIGN organization performs:

1. Functional Specification
2. Software Design Reviews
3. Hardware/Software Interface
4. S/W Document Audit
5. S/W Requirement Allocation

The SYSTEM EFFECTIVENESS organization is responsible for:

1. Reliability
2. Quality
3. Maintainability Requirements
4. Human Factors

The SYSTEM STANDARDS, PLANNING AND AUDIT organization is charged with:

1. Establishing Software Standards
2. System Standards Planning
3. Program Audit

The CORPORATE OPERATIONS PLANNING organization performs:

1. Major Program Planning
2. Corporate Architecture Planning
3. Establishing Computing Policy

As you can see, this is a very extensive list of activities and will be expensive to do. Only very large organization motivated by other large organizations like the Department of Defense can do them. But, the idea is that whether the system is a product or the business enterprise that produced it, certain considerations similar to the ones Appleton suggests ought to be done before giving projects their marching orders. Underlying these is a consensus about managing the complexity of the systems with which we have to deal today. Deciding to pay attention to the list above helps brings to the surface most of the important issues. It is expensive, yes, but I suppose its a case of "pay me now or pay me later."

System Engineering is an umbrella activity under which software development and other business activities take place. System Engineering isn't much thought of explicitly as a separate field of study yet. Engineers from various disciplines arrive at System Engineering from their native disciplines. For example, a traffic-control engineer becomes a Systems Engineer when he analyzes and designs for traffic patterns.

There are indications, however, that the kinds of activities that go on in System Engineering are now being given more weight. Enterprise models, corporate data dictionaries, data naming standards, and the Jackson System Design view of development as a mapping of business activities to the eventual software system all indicate that there is a growing awareness of the value of the bigger picture that System Engineering can provide.

Summary

These, then, are ways we organize ourselves to do software development in our current milieu. They range from formal to informal, impersonal to very personal, and from humongous to human scale. They all have their place. But, that place resides in an environment that is struggling to become respectable. In the next chapter, I will describe that environment and what we can do about it.

CHAPTER NINE
Professionalism and Science

Professionalism

I talked earlier about the problems of establishing professionalism in our field. In this area, more than anywhere, I believe we are different. We don't know who we are yet. In this chapter, I will discuss the state of our professionalism and science, and offer some things we can do to improve them.

Remember the anecdote from Chapter Four about a knowledgeable user having trouble with a new system, because she thought it was 'designed for programmers'? Let us explore that complaint and others like it.

And, I have four complaints of my own. These occur in other fields but, as far as I can tell, they are rampant in ours. The reason for this can be traced directly to the missing professionalism.

Deep but Narrow Knowledge

Most of us in software engineering work in areas where we specialize in a few things and get them down pat. We develop deep but narrow knowledge and experience. COBOL programmers rarely talk to FORTRAN guys. We know a great deal about a few things. Often, we come to our jobs with training in another field, say accounting or physics, and train just enough for the activity at hand.

Sometimes we are promoted based on our performance. Often, however, a promotion requires much wider knowledge than we possess. And, sometimes we don't know that.

Some examples are the folks in data centers who are promoted into positions where distributed processing is going on, accounting computing experts promoted into positions where scientific programming is also happening, and software folks promoted into positions where hardware and telecommunication are also involved.

My complaint is that we are not given a basis in our training for adjusting to these new situations. Our training is also narrow and deep.

Management is faced with a tough problem. It has to select the best candidates for promotion from those with deep but narrow knowledge. Often when this happens, those who are promoted behave in accordance with past experience. But, this past experience is no longer relevant.

In a distributed computing environment, the new manager from the data center will install new software that brings down the whole shop. This might seem normal, though unfortunate, to him, but extremely abnormal and frustrating to the users who expect their workstations to be isolated from problems elsewhere in the system.

A former business software person will attempt to apply business methods (like the Waterfall approach) to scientific areas in which Handcuffing is the predominant development approach.

A software guy will be sold the wrong equipment because he depends on the vendor to solve his hardware problems.

Do you think this is baloney? Well, I have seen every one of these situations, and more. My environment is not so special. Colleagues and acquaintances from many companies, laboratories, and organizations report similar circumstances.

It is important for us to learn our jobs well, but we should be equipped to transfer what is relevant to other posts and to have ways of adjusting to new circumstances. Our education should provide the hooks. But it doesn't.

The Curse of the Power User

In this deep and narrow world lives a type of developer known as a "power user." You know who they are and, most of the time, they are not evil. In fact, they are usually pretty nice folks and very hard workers. Often, they work on solving difficult problems and have a firm grasp of them in their heads.

Nevertheless, they could use help and are alert for it. When something new comes along, they give it a try. If it makes producing their program easier for them, they get interested. They learn the tool. It might have some foibles or might not be well formed, but they can see through these difficulties to the possibilities. So, they become expert users—power users.

The power users learn all the ins and outs of the tool. They learn all of the short cuts and how to avoid the pitfalls. They begin to identify with the tool and see it as an answer to all of the problems in their world, which is deep but narrow.

They switch from being users to being advocates. They join together to form "Users Groups." If there is a vendor, power users develop close ties with him. The vendor, in turn, encourages this with free or low cost seminars and other activities. The power users become the vendor's user base. Efforts are made to spread the tool throughout the environment. Sometimes it becomes the "standard."

Soon, a hierarchy is formed. The vendor is on top as the purveyor of technology. Then come the loyal power users—minions in the land to be conquered. Finally come the regular people.

However, to the amazement of the power users, others, who they hoped would eagerly join the crusade to spread the creed throughout the land, do not follow. These others do not find the tool as useful. The power user's early enthusiasm begins to turn to disappointment. To buoy themselves up, conferences are held where all are invited but which are really devoted to the needs of the power users. There, vendors announce more and more features. Some of the features are not completely implemented, causing the tool to become more complex and further disenchanting regular users. But, these features attract the attention of the power users.

Vendors and power users, puzzled by the lack of universal acceptance, try new strategies. They encourage training, which they hope will overcome fear of the tool. They approach local authorities, hoping to get official endorsement for their view of the land of milk and honey.

But, general support first freezes and then evaporates leaving the power users and vendors as remnants, like a white dwarf after a nova explosion, sending frequent and regular reports to a less and less interested world.

And, what about us regular folks? We are left with the emptiness of the Chinese Lunch Syndrome. Yet another report of the Holy Grail proves false. Yet another crusade with less than complete victory.

Being good people all, we move on, sometimes reluctantly, to other fields. And the power users? Well, they stay stuck, doing their work with their tool in a small, irreducible enclave of technology.

The Khomeini Effect (The True Believer)

Among the ranks of the power users are those who burn with a desire to set the world straight. These become the Khomeinis—the true believers. They make no bones about their visions. "Do it my way or I'll kill you" is their cry. They come to meetings with their BOOK.

As power users, they continue to make claims for the goodness of their WAY, but now these are more extravagant. Intelligent, immodest, and with burning visions, very deep knowledge, and very strong, assertive personalities, they get themselves put in charge of the crusade. And heresy, the usual safety valve, is no longer tolerated. Threats are made about failure to comply with the creed. Moral judgments replace technical ones. If a project fails, those involved must seek some kind of forgiveness. "If you had only followed the Rule, this wouldn't have happened. But I know you are only a regular person and afflicted by the devil, so you are forgiven. Go and sin no more."

Because of their strong personalities, they rise to prominence in large organizations. Then, they become dangerous. They have a lot of profits to spend. They are involved in many decisions with far-reaching effects.

They dazzle you with their vision, their audacity, and their intelligence. They seem to know what they are doing. They carry on for some time until it is noticed that they do not produce much of anything. When this is pointed out to them, they produce yet another plan and start another crusade. Profits are being burned at an alarming rate. Nothing seems to be happening. After a while, something has to be done. With varying degrees of gentleness, the visionary is removed and shunted off to some backwater where his activity can be insulated from the main part of the organization.

Meanwhile, under this power user's guidance, whole new organizations have sprung up to promulgate the creed. Seminary-like, these organizations propose to train missionaries who would go forth to conquer the world for the creed. Seminars are still being held. All the trappings of officialdom, gathered to raise the priesthood to new heights of prestige and honor, still apply.

And we regular folks spend more of our time disabusing our managers of the notions of these visionaries with varying degrees of success.

Technical Decisions Made by Unqualified People

Because of the complaints I mention above, unqualified people are making important technical decisions. Take software research, for example. Here is what David Parnas has to say about it within the DoD:

"Although there are a few notable exceptions within the DoD, the majority of those who manage its applied research program are neither successful researchers nor people with extensive system building experience. There are outstanding researchers who work for DoD, but most of them work in the laboratories, not the funding agencies. There are many accomplished system builders who work for DoD, but their managers often consider them too valuable to allow them to spend their time reviewing research proposals. The people who end up making funding decisions in DoD are very often unsuccessful researchers, unsuccessful system builders, and people who enter bureaucracy immediately after their education. We call them technocrats.

"Technocrats are bombarded with weighty volumes of highly detailed proposals that they are ill prepared to judge. They do not have time to study and think; they are forced to rely on the advice of others. When they look for advice, they look for people that they know well, whether or not they are people whose areas of expertise are appropriate, and whether or not they have unbiased positions on the subject.

"Most technocrats are honest and hard-working but they are not capable of doing what is needed. The result is a very inefficient research program. I am convinced that there is now much more money being spent on software research than can be usefully spent. Very little of the work that is sponsored leads to results that are useful. Many useful results go unnoticed because the good work is buried in the rest." [Parnas 1985]

Time and again, I have also found this to be true in our field. Smart, eager, hardworking people trying to work by the rules or applying deep, narrow knowledge to areas where broader experience is needed, are getting wrapped around the axle.

We end up with the wrong hardware, the wrong software, and we fix things that "aren't broke." And managers, unable to cope, start looking for the Holy Grail. They seek it in the inventories of vendors, or in their promises, or in their vaporware. Time and again, they divert their attention from their shops to go looking for technology.

Don't get me wrong. Some very good work goes on, but I fear that most of it meets the fate that Parnas describes.

These complaints describe the features of our field that operate on the people who produced the system that was previously described as being designed for programmers—not ordinary people.

Here are two other complaints about our products, and they are whoppers. The first is from David Parnas again. "When most engineering products have been completed, tested, and sold, it is reasonable to expect that the product design is correct and that it will work reliably. With software products, it is usual to find that the software has major bugs and does not work reliably for some users. ... While most products come with an express or implied warranty, software products often carry a specific disclaimer of warranty." [Parnas 1985]

Parnas offers one reason for this: the nature of software. He sees software systems as discrete systems, with a very large numbers of states, rather than as continuous systems that are well known. He says our mathematical tools are not adequate to the job of dealing with these. Then he says, "Most designers in traditional engineering disciplines have been educated to understand the mathematical tools that are available to them. Most programmers cannot even begin to use the meager tools that are available to software engineers." [ibid]

The next complaint comes from Donald Norman. Norman is a cognitive psychologist at UCSD and the director of the Institute for Cognitive Science since 1981. He is a consultant to the computer industry on human-computer interaction and user-centered design, and has authored and edited many books and articles on the subject. In his book, "The Psychology of Everyday Things," he has this to say:

"If you set out to make something difficult to use, you could probably do no better than to copy the designers of modern computer systems. Do you want to do things wrong? Here is what to do:

"Make things invisible. Give no hints about what's expected, or about the results of what's been done.

"Be arbitrary. Use non-obvious command names and actions. Use arbitrary mapping between the intended action and what actually must be done.

"Be inconsistent. Change the rules. Let something be done one way in one mode and another way in another mode.

"Make operations unintelligible. Use idiosyncratic language or abbreviations. Use uninformative error messages.

"Be impolite. Treat erroneous actions by the user as breaches of contract. Snarl. Insult. Mumble unintelligible verbiage.

"Make operations dangerous. Allow a single erroneous action to destroy invaluable work. Make it easy to do disastrous things. But put warnings in the manual; then when people complain, you can ask, 'But didn't you read the manual?' " [Norman 1988]

So, we have all these deep yet narrow folks doing their work in a world that needs some width even if makes them a little shallow. As power users, they hope to *spread* their view. As Khomeinis, they try to *force* their view. And, many find themselves in positions where they are unable to do the job, but don't know it. We need some way of rounding the shoulders on those deep wells. We must learn to better understand the products we build and the people for whom we build them.

Another thing we might do is study other professions and how *they* solve problems. This way, we might learn how to apply their methods to solve some of our problems. And, we might find better ways to help them solve problems. Though this smacks of hanging around other professionals and hoping something might rub off, I don't think it will damage our professional standing much since there isn't much to damage.

We could also do a better job of determining the curricula for software engineering at our colleges and universities. There is some very good work being done on curricula studies at the Software Engineering Institute, but one of my correspondents reports that it is heavily influenced by academia, and "real world" considerations are given lower priority.

One of my younger correspondents described his university curriculum to me. It consisted of six or more math courses including set theory, a logic course, several 'hard' science courses, several different third-generation language courses, a systems course, an assembly language course, and several algorithm courses. This is a step in the right direction. However, this well-trained programmer is probably going to be managed for years to come by folks with much fewer qualifications.

Retraining our senior people along the lines of my younger correspondent is, in my opinion, essential, but is probably not going to happen.

There is something else we might try. Maybe we can do something about software design that takes *people* into account. I don't mean this in the usual sense where the user seems to be considered, where he is asked what he wants, plays a major role in development, forms teams to produce requirements, and becomes part of the project. I mean it in a technological way, by bringing in some science.

For example, when we are designing for a user, there are three kinds of ignorance. First, there are things the user knows about the problem that we don't (often until it is too late). Then, there are things about the problem that we know and he doesn't, and he often gets impatient with us when we have to deal with that stuff. Finally, there are things about the problem that neither of us know. Among those things are models of how the user can be expected to use the system, and here is one to consider. It also comes from Donald Norman.

He starts by describing seven stages of action for doing most things. We form a goal, which requires action. Then, we form an intention to act, figure out what actions are necessary, do the act (sounds sexy doesn't it?), check to see the effect of our act, interpret the effect and, finally, evaluate the outcome to determine whether we achieved our goal. The seven are listed below:

- forming a goal
- forming an intention to act
- specifying the action
- executing the action
- perceiving the state of the world

- interpreting the state of the world
- evaluating the outcome

We can ask questions about each of these stages. He states them in terms of using some unspecified device:

- How easily can one determine the function of the device?
- What actions are possible?
- What is the mapping from intention to physical movement?
- Should the action be performed?
- Can I tell if the system is in the desired state?
- Can I determine the mapping from system state to interpretation?
- Can I tell what state the system is in?

These resolve into four design criteria:

- **Visibility**

   "By looking, the user can tell the state of the device and the alternatives for action."

- **A good conceptual model**

   "The designer provides a good conceptual model for the user, with consistency in the presentation of operations and results and a coherent, consistent system image."

- **Good mappings**

   "It is possible to determine the relationships between actions and results, between controls and their effects, and between system state and what is visible."

- **Feedback**

   "The user receives full and continuous feedback about the results of actions."

Norman then offers suggestions about why designers go astray. First, they put aesthetics first, which might obscure visibility, feedback, and mapping and hinder the user from building a good conceptual model. Someone who doesn't need these things might assume, even unconsciously, that they aren't needed. Hell, he might not even know that they ever *were* needed. Second, designers are not typical users. They are often power users who have the operation down pat. And, the designer's clients may not be users. They could very well be the managers of the users, and not people who have direct experience with the software. The guy sitting at the desk next to you isn't likely to be a typical user either.

Norman then provides some design pointers:

- Use both knowledge in the world and knowledge in the head.

- Try to reach a balance between specifying everything and specifying nothing. In fact, achieve several options.

Some software provides much information in the world, such as a large menu structure of commands from which the user can select (information in the world); but, the menu also provides shortcuts and keystroke equivalents for the experienced user (information the user has memorized and retained in her head).

- Simplify the structure of tasks.

- Make things visible: bridge the gulfs between Execution and Evaluation.

- Get the mappings right.

- Exploit the power of constraints, both natural and artificial.

- Design for error.

- When all else fails, standardize.

"Sure," you say, "my boss would just love for me to design commands for novice, intermediate, and expert users. He is just waiting for me to question the standard screen layout we spent so many meetings developing. And, he's changed his mind about making the user remember so many codes."

Well, I know we don't really have a situation where designing to psychological models is acceptable. But, every once in a while, something like that shows up. Take the Macintosh for example.

When the Macintosh came onto the scene, business was underwhelmed. The Macintosh was considered a toy. But, it made some headway after a while, though it was upstream all the way.

However, it eventually *was* accepted, even in light of the "other machine." Let me tell you how *well* accepted. In one organization I am familiar with, there are buildings with very large, square rooms filled with desks for white-collar workers (maybe 15 desks on a side). I found myself at the wrong corner of one of these rooms and started across to the opposite corner. On most of the desks were workstations of one kind or another. I noticed that every one of the Macintoshes was turned on, and every one of the other PCs was turned off. Some of the PCs even had their keyboards placed on top of the CRT to free up more desk space.

Here is what Norman has to say: "The Macintosh provides an example of what computer systems could be like. The design emphasizes visibility and feedback. Its "human interface guidelines" and its internal "toolbox" provide standards for the many programmers who design for it. It has emphasized consideration for the user. Yes, there are several serious drawbacks to the Macintosh: it is far from perfect. And it isn't unique. Still, for its relative success in making usability and understanding into primary design objectives, I'd give the Apple Macintosh a prize. If only I thought more of prizes." [ibid]

Somehow, we have got to find a way to include ideas like Donald Norman's notions of "design" into our field.

We must locate at our center a group of ideas that explain who we are and what we are trying to do. This set then becomes the core of our professionalism. We ought to find common ground upon which we can build our discipline. COBOLers should be allowed to talk with FORTRANers. And, if we had something about the world to explain, maybe we could begin to talk the same language.

Science

I have tried to describe the things I have seen in our field of computing through the mists of our current environment. And, to the extent they are interesting, I leave it to others to verify my observations and make sense of them. I might be viewing the canals on Mars; I am not a scientist and don't intend to be one.

Rather, I am an interested lay person of the kind that supported significant scientific theorizing in the past, such as that in the fields of astronomy and biological evolution.

But, I want to speculate on science for our field. Up until now, our field has been a hodge podge of parts of other sciences, much as an alchemist mixed things together to produce shining gold.

Let me begin by explaining where I think science fits in. Technology is composed of two things: science and engineering. Science abstracts and analyzes parts of the world and explains it to us using well-known rules. Engineering synthesizes the things that are discovered and isolated by science into useful objects for all of us, including scientists.

Here are some observations about science and our field.

It has become increasingly important in science to take the observer into account. [See Stephen Jay Gould's *The Mismeasure of Man*, 1981; and references to Hiesenberg's uncertainty principle in the literature] Computing has always served to extend humanity's mental functions. Humans, as observers, are being well served by computing.

Maybe our theory and what we have to say about the world is to describe the observer of the world. That seems to be where we are heading. More and more, a variety of our mental functions are being synthesized in the laboratory, such as memory, vision, hearing, speech, and language. Indeed, there are (or were) great sums of money put into Artificial Intelligence.

Expert systems and knowledge-based systems have found application, and these fields seem to be growing. The computer has become the metaphor for the brain, as in memory and processing based on logic and mathematics. And, software has become the metaphor for the operation of the brain.

When I learned programming, it was suggested that we think of the computer as a dumb servant who will do anything we ask, but we must tell it everything, every step along the way. (This might be changing with 4GLs and nonprocedural languages.)

Finally, we see the mind emerging from the operation of the brain. But, we have no metaphor for it yet. And, that is where I believe we will find our science.

Scientific theories are often shocking, and I have one of those to sketch. It explains no less than the origin of consciousness. It comes from Julian Jaynes, a teacher of psychology at Princeton University. He presents his theory in a book entitled *The Origin of Consciousness in the Breakdown of the Bicameral Mind.* [1976]

He starts by giving a short history of past attempts to explain consciousness. But, then he makes some startling claims about what consciousness is *not*. It is not necessary for reactivity (responsiveness to stimuli). Nor is it involved in the performance of a skill. In fact, it often hinders it. It need not be involved in speaking, writing, listening, or reading. It does not copy down experience. It is not *at all* involved in signal learning and need not be involved in the learning of skills or solutions. It is not necessary for making judgments or in simple thinking. It is not the seat of reason and it has no location, except an imaginary one.

Important to his theory is the notion of metaphor and analog. Metaphor is a way of creating new knowledge with old knowledge. Jaynes decomposes the term into two parts: the metaphier, which is the old knowledge, and the metaphrand, which is the new knowledge to be created with the old. (See Figure 9-1.)

He further decomposes each of these into terms that provide nuances: paraphier and paraphrand respectively. He gives an example: "Consider the metaphor that the snow blankets the ground. The metaphrand is something about the completeness and even thickness with which the ground is covered by the snow. The metaphier is a blanket on the bed. But the pleasing nuances of this metaphor are in the paraphiers of the metaphier, blanket. These are something about warmth protection and slumber until some period of awakening. These associations of blanket then automatically become the associations or paraphrands of the original metaphrand, like the way snow covers the ground. And thus we have created by this metaphor the idea of the earth sleeping and protected by the snow cover until its awakening in spring. All this is packed into the simple use of the word blanket to pertain to the way snow covers the ground." [Jaynes 1976]

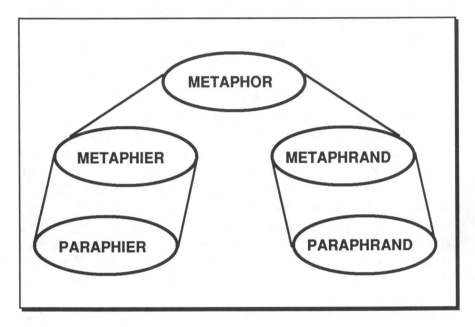

Figure 9-1. The Composition of a Metaphor

Jaynes then defines consciousness as a kind of model called an analog. An analog is a special model. Where models, such as scientific models, are used to give explanation or understanding, "analogs are constructed from something well-known if not completely known." [ibid] Maps are a good example.

"Subjective Conscious mind is an analog of what is called the real world. It is built up with a vocabulary or lexical field whose terms are all metaphors or analogs of behavior in the physical world. Its reality is of the same order as mathematics. It allows us to shortcut behavioral processes and arrive at more adequate decisions. Like mathematics it is an operator rather then a thing or repository And it is intimately bound up with volition and decision.

"Consciousness is the metaphrand when it is being generated by the paraphrands of our verbal expressions. But the functioning of consciousness is as it were the return journey ... [it] becomes the metaphier full of our past experience, constantly and selectively operating on such unknowns as future action, decisions, and partly remembered pasts, on what we are and yet may be." [ibid]

For Jaynes, consciousness is man's adapting to the breakdown of the bicameral mind. He says, "... ancient people from Mesopotamia to Peru could not think as we do today, and were therefore not conscious. Unable to introspect, they experienced auditory hallucinations—voices of gods actually heard as in the Old Testament or the Iliad—which, coming from the brain's right hemisphere, told a person what to do in circumstances of novelty or stress. This ancient mentality is called the bicameral mind." [ibid]

He then argues that several things served to break down this state of affairs.

- The power of auditory perception was weakened by the advent of writing.

- Hallucinatory control is inherently fragile.

- Gods don't seem to work in the chaos of historical upheaval.

- The mixing of vast numbers of people due to catastrophe.

- The acquisition of a kind of history in the epics.

- The need to deceive and natural selection.

As these became too much, the bicameral mind broke down. People adjusted to this by inventing consciousness, this metaphorizing of the world in order to survive.

I don't know what the current state of the theory is and even Jaynes hasn't worked it out completely, at least in his first book. But, it is a theory and it makes claims that can be tested about a metaphor-generated model of the world. Maybe someday, somebody with a computer will do the test. I expect something of the sort will happen. Because, with all of the talk about how to write software and how to use it, with all of the arrows of our work pointing back to us, I have a hunch that we become our theory. That ultimately, we seek ourselves in a proximate mirror.

ABOUT THE AUTHORS:

Peter DeGrace is a former programmer trained in COBOL and Fortran who ended up in a software engineering reference library. There, he discovered many problems, questions, and answers about software development and software engineering, including how people "do" software. This book is the result of a lot of thinking about what he has learned, and about what software developers do and how they do it.

Peter's education and experience includes data processing, COBOL and Fortran programming, systems analysis, software development, CASE tools, software methodologies, economics, and 20th century thought and expression.

Peter is a MENSAn, which may explain why he *enjoys* studying economics (especially labor theory), anything related to the computer field, living in the Pacific Northwest, music (which he discovered late in life), fine art (which he discovered early in life), and playing with his two dogs, Desdemona and Cleopatra.

Leslie Hulet Stahl is a technical writer (hardware and software reference and user's manuals), editor, illustrator, and consultant in the electronic publishing and CAD/CAM fields. One of her recent software user's guides won an award from the Society for Technical Communications. As an independent technical writer and editor, she provided writing and editing services for such companies as IBM and Boeing Computer Services. As owner and Editor-in-Chief of Documents Unlimited Company (which landed her in Who's Who in the West) she provided desktop publishing and editing services for many clients worldwide.

When she isn't working on books with Peter, Leslie enjoys writing horror fiction; playing computer games, Scrabble, and progressive Rummy; and her pets: Bruno (generic Dog), Grunt (purebred Great Dane), Arielle and Chuckie (basic Cockatiels), Bert and Ernie (Amazon parrots), and most of all David (pedigreed husband).

BIBLIOGRAPHY

Agresti, W.W., 1986. "Introduction to Part IV, Operational Specification," p.99, from *New Paradigms for Software Development,* Tutorial. Edited by William Agresti. Published by IEEE Computer Society Press.

Agresti, W.W., 1986. "The Operational versus the Conventional Approach to Software Development," p.108, from *New Paradigms for Software Development,* Tutorial. Edited by William Agresti. Published by IEEE Computer Society Press.

Agresti, W.W., 1986. "What Are the New Paradigms?" from *New Paradigms for Software Development,* Tutorial. Edited by William Agresti. Published by IEEE Computer Society Press.

Appleton, D.S., 1986. "Very Large Projects," pp.62-64, *Datamation,* Vol. 32, No. 2, January 1986, Cahners Publishing Company.

Blum, B.I., 1987. "GAO Report FGMSD-80-4 Revisited," p.49, *ACM SIGSOFT Software Engineering Notes,* Vol. 12, No. 1, January 1987.

Boehm, B.W., 1985. "A Spiral Model of Software Development and Enhancement," from *Proceedings of an International Workshop on the Software Process and Software Environments,* Coto de Caza, Trabuco Canyon, California, March 27-29, 1985. Edited by Jack C. Wileden and Mark Downson. Sponsored by ACM Sigsoft and IEEE-TCSE. Proceedings ACM SIGSOFT.

Boehm, B.W., 1981. "Software Engineering Economics," p.4, reprinted by permission of Prentice Hall, Inc., Englewood Cliffs, NJ.

Boehm, B.W., T.E. Gray, and T. Seewaldt, 1984. "Prototyping Versus Specifying: A Multiproject Experiment," *IEEE Transactions on Software Engineering,* Vol. SE-10, No. 3, May 1984.

Bronowski, J., 1973. "The Ascent of Man," p.360, Little, Brown and Company.

Brooks, F.P., Jr., 1987. "No Silver Bullet: Essence and Accidents of Software Engineering," *Computer,* April 1987, published by IEEE Computer Society.

Brooks, F.P., Jr., 1975. "The Mythical Man-Month," Addison-Wesley.

Cameron, J.R., 1986. "An Overview of JSD," *IEEE Transactions on Software Engineering,* Vol. SE-12, No. 2, February 1986.

Card, D.N., F.E. McGarry, and G.T. Page, 1987. "Evaluating Software Engineering Technologies," *IEEE Transactions on Software Engineering,* Vol. SE-13, No. 7, July 1987.

Case, A.F., Jr., 1987. "Structured Analysis and Design: The Evolution of a Methodology," *System Development,* Vol. 7, No. 8, August 1987.

Cioch, F.A., 1988. "An Audiovisual Document for Software Maintenance," Conference on Software Maintenance (CSM-88), October 24-27, 1988, Phoenix, AZ (Maintenance), from *System Development,* Applied Computer Research, Inc.

Dyer, M. and H.D. Mills, 1981. "The Cleanroom Approach to Reliable Software Development," in *Proc. Validation Methods Research for Fault-Tolerant Avionics and Control Systems Sub-Working Group Meeting: Production of Reliable Flight-Crucial Software,* Research Triangle Institute, North Carolina, Nov. 2-4, 1981.

Gilchrist, T. et al, "Incremental System Development—A Tutorial," DOC #BCS-G2850, Boeing Computer Services, Seattle, WA, 1989.

Gladden, G.R., 1982. "Stop the Life-Cycle, I Want to Get Off," *ACM SIGSOFT Software Engineering Notes,* Vol. 7, No. 3, April 1982 (Development).

Goldsheider, L., 1962. "A Survey of Michelangelo's Models in Wax and Clay," Phaidon Press, Ltd., London. Quoting from, respectively, Vasari, 1550, Introduction to Sculpture, prefix to "Lives of the Artists"; and Giovanni Battista Armenini, 1587, "Precetti della Pittura (Ravenna)."

Gould, S.J., 1981. "The Mismeasure of Man," W.W. Norton & Co.

Harvey, J.B., "The Abilene Paradox: The Management of Agreement," pp. 16-43, *Organizational Dynamics,* Vol. 17, No. 1, Summer 1988, American Management Association, AMACOM.

Henken, P., CPA, 1988. "Improving Structured Systems Analysis with Video," *Journal of Systems Management,* May 1988 (Analysis).

Jaynes, J., 1976. "The Origin of Consciousness in the Breakdown of the Bicameral Mind," Houghton Mifflin Company.

Kidder, T., 1982. "The Soul of a New Machine," Avon Books.

Lammers, S., 1986. "Programmers at Work," Microsoft Press.

Lantz, K.E., 1987. "The Prototyping Methodology," p.10, adapted by permission of Prentice Hall, Inc., Englewood Cliffs, NJ.

Ledgard, H., 1987. "Professional Software: Software Engineering Concepts," pp.5-12, Addison-Wesley Publishing Company.

Martin, J., and C. McClure, 1985. "Diagramming Techniques for Analysts and Programmers," Prentice-Hall.

Martin, J., 1985. "Fourth-Generation Languages," Volume I, Prentice Hall.

Mathis, R.F., 1986. "The Last 10 Percent," *IEEE Transactions on Software Engineering,* Vol. SE-12, No. 6, September 1986.

McCracken, D.D., and M.A. Jackson, 1986. "A Minority Dissenting Position," pp.23-25, from *New Paradigms for Software Development,* Tutorial. Edited by William Agresti. Published by IEEE Computer Society Press.

McCracken, D.D., and M.A. Jackson, 1982. "Life Cycle Concept Considered Harmful," *ACM SIGSOFT Software Engineering Notes,* Vol. 7, No. 2, April 1982.

McFarland, G., 1986. "The Benefits of Bottom Up Design," *ACM SIGSOFT Software Engineering Notes,* Vol. 11, No. 5, October 1986.

Norman, D.A., 1988. "The Psychology of Everyday Things," Basic Books, subsidiary of Harper and Row.

Parnas, D.L., 1985. "Software Aspects of Strategic Defense Systems," *American Scientist,* Vol. 73, September-October 1985, Sigma Xi, The Scientific Research Society.

Peters, L., 1983. "The 'Chinese Lunch' Syndrome in Software Engineering Education: Causes and Remedies," IEEE Computer Society Workshop on Software Engineering Technology Transfer, April 25-27, 1983.

Rickert, N.W., "The Parable of Two Programmers," p.16, Department of Mathematics, Statistics, and Computer Science, University of Chicago at Illinois, from *ACM SIGSOFT Software Engineering Notes,* Vol. 10, No. 1, January 1985.

Rittel, H., and M. Webber, 1973. "Dilemmas in a General Theory of Planning," pp.155-169, *Policy Sciences,* Vol. 4, Elsevier Scientific Publishing Company, Inc., Amsterdam (printed in Scotland), a subsidiary of Elsevier Space NDU NV.

Sagan, C., 1974. "Broca's Brain," p.235, Ballantine Books.

Seckel, A., and J. Edwards, 1986. "The Revolt Against the Lightning Rod," *Free Inquiry,* Vol. 6, No. 3, Summer 1986.

Selby, R.W., Jr., V.R. Basili, and F.T. Baker, 1987. "Cleanroom Software Development: An Empirical Evaluation," *IEEE Transactions on Software Engineering,* Vol. SE-13, No. 9, September 1987.

Shere, K., 1988. "Software Engineering and Management," pp.28-31, Prentice Hall.

Takeuchi, T., and I. Nonaka, 1986. "The New New Product Development Game," *Harvard Business Review,* January-February 1986.

Vessey, I. and R. Weber, 1984. "Research on Structured Programming: An Empiricist's Evaluation," *IEEE Transactions on Software Engineering,* Vol. SE-10, No. 4, July 1984.

Yourdon, E. and L.L. Constantine, 1977. "Structured Design," preface by L.L. Constantine, Yourdon Press.

Zave, P., 1986. "The Operational versus the Conventional Approach to Software Development," from *New Paradigms for Software Development,* Tutorial. Edited by William Agresti. Published by IEEE Computer Society Press.

Zelkowitz, M.V., 1988. "Resource Utilization During Software Development." pp.331,336, *The Journal of Systems and Software,* No. 8, Elsevier Science Publishing Co., Inc.

Additional references:

"A Programmer's Productivity Controversy," EDP Analyzer, Canning Publications.

"Guidelines for Writing Gibbs Programs," Cornell University, Center for Theory and Simulation in Science and Engineering, October 1984.

"Productivity in Computer Applications Development," Burroughs Corporation, LINC Corporate Program Management.

"System Engineering Management Guide," public domain, available through any Government Printing Office, Stock No. 008-020-01099-5, 1986.

Britannica World Language Edition of Funk and Wagnells Standard Dictionary, 1963. Vol. 1, p.246, col. 3, Funk and Wagnalls Company.

Clip art is used by permission of T/Maker Company. ClickArt® is a registered trademark of T/Maker Co.©, 1987.

DOD-HDBK-287.

DOD-STD-7935, 15 February 1983.

GAO Report FGMSD-80-4, summarized in a footnote in *IEEE Transactions on Software Engineering,* p.38, Vol. SE-10, No. 4, July 1984.

System Development Life Cycle, as it appears in DOD-STD-2167, 4 June 1985.

INDEX

References are to page numbers. Page numbers that are shown in **bold italics** indicate illustrations.

The titles of illustrations, articles, and books are shown in *italics*. Illustrations are listed under the heading "Illustrations," alphabetically arranged by abbreviated titles and key concepts. Please refer to the Table of Contents for a complete listing of all illustrations, and to the Bibliography for a complete, descriptive listing of the works of all indexed authors.

We appreciate your taking the time to fill this out. —
Peter and Leslie

Was the material organized properly?

☐ YES ☐ NO. I think it should be arranged ... —————
_____
_____

Are any of the ideas incorrect (or are they just controversial)?

☐ NO ☐ I'M NOT SURE ☐ JUST CONTROVERSIAL

☐ YES (Please provide page number and clarification. Send us
a letter explaining your views if there is not enough space
here.) _____

_____

_____

Do you feel the need to burn us at the stake for heresy?

☐ YES ☐ NO ☐ UNDECIDED

Have you seen other transformations of the Waterfall that we could
add to our bestiary?

☐ NO ☐ YES, AND HERE IT IS (or here they are) ——————
_____

_____

Were there enough graphics to adequately illustrate the material?

☐ YES ☐ NO ☐ UNDECIDED

Did you enjoy the book?

☐ YES ☐ NO ☐ UNDECIDED

Any Other Comments?

_____
_____
_____
_____

CUT ALONG HERE

DeGrace and Stahl
24316 SE 473rd Street
Enumclaw, WA 98022